SCIENCE, POLITICS AND GNOSTICISM

TWO ESSAYS

The first essay, "Science, Politics and Gnosticism," was translated by William J. Fitzpatrick. The second essay, "Ersatz Religion," first appeared in German in *Wort und Wahrheit* and in English in *Politeia*.

ISBN 978-0-89526-419-0

Library of Congress Cataloging-in-Publication Data

Voegelin, Eric, 1901–
    [Wissenschaft, Politik, und Gnosis. English]
    Science, politics, and gnosticism : two essays / Eric Voegelin.
        p.   cm.
    Originally published: Chicago, 1968.
    Includes bibliographical references and index.
    Contents: Science, politics and gnosticism—Ersatz religion.
    ISBN 0-89526-419-6
        1. Political science. 2. Gnosticism. I. Voegelin, Eric, 1901–
Ersatz religion. 1997. II. Title.
JC233.V6413 1997
320'.01—dc21   97–13501
                                                                        CIP

Published in the United States by
Gateway Editions, an imprint of
Regnery Publishing
A Division of Salem Media Group
300 New Jersey Ave NW
Washington, DC 20001
www.Regnery.com

Printed on acid-free paper.
Manufactured in the United States of America

2018 Printing

SCIENCE, POLITICS AND GNOSTICISM

TWO ESSAYS

BY ERIC VOEGELIN

With a New Introduction by

ELLIS SANDOZ
Louisiana State University

Gateway Editions
REGNERY PUBLISHING
WASHINGTON, D.C.

CONTENTS

INTRODUCTION

I T IS WITH PLEASURE that I write a few lines of introduction to Eric
Voegelin's *Science, Politics and Gnosticism*. In the period since it
first appeared in German in 1959, and was later translated by
Henry Regnery in 1968, it has become a classic of modern political theory. It demonstrates the power of Voegelin's thought, his lu-
cidity of expression, and his unique and cogent analysis of the
demonic in modern existence. It also shows that the new science of
politics, indebted to classical and Christian philosophy, can be used
to diagnose the maladies of contemporary political existence and
offer remedies within the modest limits of reason and science. In
this brief introduction I should like to reflect on the character of
Voegelin's analysis, its common sense, as well as its philosophical
foundations. In addition, I wish to suggest the place of the material,
as presented here, in the larger scheme of Voegelin's philosophy of
human affairs.

Let me say first that the present volume extends and deepens the
thesis of the latter part of *The New Science of Politics* (1952) that the
"essence of modernity is Gnosticism." It also continues to display
the "new science," which is anchored in ordinary experience and
utilizes the Aristotelian method. The nub of the latter is the great
strength of Voegelin's philosophy. He begins with commonsense
understanding of the issue at hand as a given and then ascends ana-
lytically, clarifying the key experiences of reality in which every man
shares and through which he becomes—if he is philosophically inclined and moved by reason—a partner in the inquiry of truth.

The first part of the work, initially delivered as the inaugural lecture of the new professor of political science at the University of Munich on November 26, 1958, deals with the modern crisis of human existence intelligibly and brilliantly. The talk of "Gnosticism," however, is not immediately accessible until some of the particulars come into view. But this is no more than a momentary obstacle to understanding. Those with a background in Voegelin's thought need no introduction to the present material, so I shall address those who are less familiar with his work.

The context of Voegelin's discourse is a philosopher's search for truth and his personal resistance to untruth in its manifold forms, especially as untruth affects the political situation from which his philosophizing takes its impetus. There is nothing pretentious in this. For Voegelin believed that the vocation of the philosopher had much in common with the vocation of all other human beings, and he spelled out this belief in an early passage of his Antrittsvorlesung (inaugural lecture). As his principal philosophical mentor Plato contended, the philosopher is no more than an exemplary human being—not a species apart. Therefore, in addressing his new colleagues and the assembled students of the University of Munich on a solemn occasion, Voegelin clarified the subject matter and truth of his discourse as applicable to each and everyone present— as well as to prospective readers—as follows:

> We shall now try to present the phenomenon of the prohibition of questions through an analysis of representative opinions. Thus, this effort will present not only the phenomenon, but the exercise of analysis as well. It should show that the spiritual disorder of our time, the civilizational crisis of which everyone so readily speaks, does not by any means have to be borne as an inevitable fate; . . . on the contrary, everyone possesses the means of overcoming it in his own life. And our effort [here] should not only indicate the means, but also show

how to employ them. No one is obliged to take part in the spiritual crisis of a society; on the contrary, everyone is obliged to avoid this folly and live his life in order. Our presentation of the phenomenon, therefore, will at the same time furnish the remedy for it through therapeutic analysis (15).

Thus, he evokes the philosopher as physician of the soul. One commentator, reflecting on the overall character of Voegelin's philosophizing, offers these helpful remarks:

> To understand Voegelin's philosophy of order-disorder, it is necessary to recognize that his philosophy is the protest of good against evil. . . . Behind Voegelin the historian is Voegelin the prophet crying, "Woe unto them that call evil good and good evil" (Isa. 5:20). The judgments upon the kinds of philosophy available involve sorting out the evil from the good. The powerful forms politically have been fascist (including the worst variety of the Nazis) and communist; and the degenerate or "derailed" modern philosophy has only feeble protests against collectivist tyrannies of Right and Left. The bad forms are very bad, and Voegelin has no nice academic party manners that inhibit him from calling Karl Marx a "swindler" and his master, Hegel, a charlatan who played "con games". . . . By "true" philosophy Voegelin means basically good philosophy. It is classical and Christian, the heritage of Plato, Aristotle, St. Augustine, out of whom came St. Thomas Aquinas and scholasticism. . . . The conception Voegelin has of good and true philosophy is so noble that any practicing philosopher would tremble to try to do more than suggest what it is. Philosophy, which has the role of saving us from evil, is "the love of being through love of divine Being as the source of its order" (*OH I,* xiv). I call Voegelin an "Augustinian" because philosophy must develop "pairs of

concepts which cast light on both good and evil" (*OH III*, 68–69). Voegelin presents a City of God against and above the City of Man. The social function of true philosophy is to resist disorder and form the community that "lives through the ages". . . .[1]

Protecting philosophy against perversion is vital to the larger task of protecting human existence itself against perversion and tyranny. The issues are matters of life and death (*OH I*, xiii). To illustrate this point, Voegelin juxtaposes famous philosophers like Marx, Comte, and Hegel, who prohibited questions that might undermine their systems' credibility, with Rudolf Höss, the commandant of the extermination camp at Auschwitz, who testified to the inability of an SS officer to ask questions in a newspaper interview a few weeks before Voegelin's lecture. No SS leader would even think of questioning his orders. "'Something like that was just completely impossible,'" said Höss. "This is very close to the wording of Marx's declaration," Voegelin wrote, "that for 'socialist man' such a question 'becomes a practical impossibility.' Thus, we see delineated three major types for whom a human inquiry has become a practical impossibility: socialist man (in the Marxian sense), positivist man (in the Comtean sense), and national-socialist man" (18).

The line drawn in the material before us is mainly between philosophy and anti-philosophy in the form of Gnosticism. What are the differences between the two? Voegelin states the two principles as follows: "Philosophy springs from the love of being; it is man's loving endeavor to perceive the order of being and attune himself to it. Gnosis desires dominion over being; in order to seize control

---

1 Paul Grimley Kuntz, "Voegelin's Experiences of Disorder Out of Order and Vision of Order Out of Disorder. . . ," in *Eric Voegelin's Significance for the Modern Mind,* ed. Ellis Sandoz (Baton Rouge, 1991), 115, 117. Cf. Ellis Sandoz, *The Voegelinian Revolution: A Biographical Introduction* (Baton Rouge, 1981), 141–42.

of being the gnostic constructs his system. The building of systems is a gnostic form of reasoning, not a philosophical one" (30). First, last, and always, philosophy is the love of wisdom, not its possession, as in the system and claim to *actual knowledge (wirkliches Wissen)* in Hegel's *Phenomenology*. The closure against divine reality—variously effected through the *libido dominandi,* or will to power, appearing as philosophy by means of systems construction, the prohibition of pertinent questions, and the murder of God—is that in modern thought which allows, first, the evocation of the autonomous Man, and, finally, the conjuring of the pretended superman *(Übermensch).* Voegelin analyzes such intentional falsifications of reality and perversions of philosophy in terms of Gnosticism in its various forms.

This book explains in considerable detail just why this is so. Does Voegelin really contend that modern ideological mass movements and the dominant "philosophical" schools are in some sense continuations of the various anti-Christian, Gnostic sects, which were discredited as heretical in antiquity—e.g., the Manicheans and Valentinians? Yes, he does. He argues that there is both an historical continuity and an experiential equivalence between the ancient movements and such modern phenomena as positivism, Marxism, Freudianism, existentialism, progressivism, utopianism, revolutionary activism, fascism, communism, national socialism, and the rest of the "isms." Aside from tracing the historical ties through substantial scholarship, which demonstrates that much of modern thought is rooted in Gnosticism, we have the experiential analysis. The latter hinges on two related experiences—alienation from a hostile world, and rebellion against the divine Ground of being.

In consequence, the leading attributes of modern Gnosticism, which arise from a lust for power, are: (1) immanentist programs to transform the world; and (2) atheism and the deification of Man as superman, master of nature, and maker of history in the wake of the death of God. Modern Gnosticism is especially distinguished from

ancient Gnosticism by its renunciation of "vertical" or other-
worldly transcendence and its proclamation of a "horizontal" transcendence or futuristic parousia of Being (Heidegger)—that is,
intramundane or worldly salvific doctrines—as ultimate truth.
Modern Gnosticism thus takes the form of speculating on the
meaning of history construed as a closed process manipulated by
the revolutionary elite—the few who understand the path, process,
and goal of history as its moves from stage to stage toward some
sort of final perfect realm (Hegel, Marx, Comte, National
Socialism). This radical immanentization or secularization of
reality means that the question of "reality" underlies all lesser issues.
This fact, in turn, gives rise to Voegelin's utilization of the symbol
"Second Reality"—the dream-world constructs of the Gnostic
ideologues whose closure against divine Being, or exclusion of
troublesome aspects of reality through forbidding questions—mu-
tilate and falsify the consciousness of reality as commonly experienced. The flavor and depth of Voegelin's thought emerges
powerfully in the following passage from his second essay, "The
Murder of God":

> The aim of parousiastic gnosticism [as in Marx, Nietzsche,
> and Heidegger] is to destroy the order of being, which is ex-
> perienced as defective and unjust, and through man's creative
> power to replace it with a perfect and just order. Now, how-
> ever the order of being may be understood—as a world dom-
> inated by cosmic-divine powers in the civilizations of the
> Near East, or as the creation of a world-transcendent God in
> Judaeo-Christian symbolism, or as an essential order of being
> in philosophical contemplation—it remains something that is
> given, that is not under man's control. In order, therefore,
> that the attempt to create a new world may seem to make
> sense, the givenness of the order of being must be obliterated;
> the order of being must be interpreted, rather, as essentially

under man's control. And taking control of being further requires that the transcendent origin of being be obliterated: it
requires the decapitation of being—the murder of God"
(35-36).

The Crucifixion of Christ as the murder of God in Hegel's
thought, for instance, is not an event but the feat of a dialectician.
The "substance of the order of being which, for the [true] philosopher, is something given is systematically construed as a succession
of phases of consciousness which proceed in dialectical development. . . . God has died because he was no more than a phase of
consciousness that is now outmoded. . . . [T]he spirit as system requires the murder of God; and, conversely, in order to commit the
murder of God the system is fashioned" (46-48).

Reductionism, transformation of the world, and construction of
ideological systems in Thomas More, Thomas Hobbes, and Hegel
figure prominently in the diagnosis of "pneumopathology" (70) in
the concluding essay, "*Ersatz* Religion: The Gnostic Mass
Movements of Our Time." This piece was not part of the original
1959 German edition but first appeared in *Wort und Wahrheit* about
a year later. It largely summarizes and elaborates the argument in
the fourth chapter of *The New Science of Politics*. In identifying the
leading characteristics of Gnosticism, Voegelin stresses that
"Knowledge—gnosis—of the method of altering being is the central concern of the gnostic" (60).

This obsession with changing the world—an exercise in futility
with disastrous consequences for mankind—is repeatedly coun-

2. This stance of Voegelin's is directly challenged by the Marquette University
theologian Robert M. Doran in "Theology's Situation: Questions to Eric Voegelin,"
The Beginning and the Beyond, Papers from the Gadamer and Voegelin Conferences,
Supplementary Issue of *Lonergan Workshop,* vol. 4, ed. Fred Lawrence (Chico, Calif.,
1984), 82-83. Important issues are here at stake that cannot be explored further in the
present context or apart from a consideration of Voegelin's later writings.

tered by Voegelin's insistence on the stability and givenness of reality. This point must be underscored: the only reality is reality experienced.[2] Therefore, the utopia of More is possible only by extracting sin (*superbia*, pride of life) from human nature—which More knew was an impossibility, hence utopian, even if subsequent utopians did not. Hobbes builds his system in *Leviathan* by obscuring reality and denying any *summum bonum*, relying instead upon the *summum malum* of violent death as his first principle. Hegel's system is contrived only by playing the game of dialectic—the unfolding of consciousness to an end of history understood as the identity of the human logos and divine Logos in the person of Hegel himself—thereby falsifying the mystery of history which is unknowable, since it extends into an opaque and indefinite future.[3] What alternatives to the "demonic mendacity" (23) of these ingenious but demonstrably, and intentionally false, "solutions" to the problems of existence does our philosopher proffer? Philosophy and faith considered experientially, in Voegelin's account, yield alternatives that lack the dogmatic certitude of the Gnostic doctrines. After analyzing the meaning of Christian faith and before considering the

---

3. Voegelin's wrestlings with Hegel run through much of his later work up to and including the final volume of *Order and History*, vol. 5, *In Search of Order* (Baton Rouge, 1987). Noteworthy is "On Hegel: A Study in Sorcery" [1971] in *Collected Works of Eric Voegelin*, vol. 12, *Published Essays 1966-1985*, ed. Ellis Sandoz (Baton Rouge, 1990), 213-255. His general relationship to German Idealism is insightfully discussed by Jürgen Gebhardt, "Toward the Process of Universal Mankind," in *Eric Voegelin's Thought: A Critical Appraisal*, ed. Ellis Sandoz (Durham, N. C., 1982), 67-86. No attempt is made here systematically to cite the relevant work by and about Voegelin on the matters at issue in this little volume. A comprehensive bibliography and guide to this literature is available, however, in Geoffrey L. Price, *Eric Voegelin: A Classified Bibliography, Bulletin of the John Ryland's University Library of Manchester*, 76 (Summer 1994), 1-180. This bibliography is updated electronically from time to time through E-mail; for information apply to Professor Price as follows: <g.price@manchester.ac.uk>.

experiences of transcendence in Judaism, philosophy, and Islam, he summarizes as follows:

> The temptation to fall from uncertain truth into certain un-truth is stronger in the clarity of Christian faith than in other spiritual structures. But the absence of a secure hold on real-ity and the demanding spiritual strain are generally character-istic of border experiences in which man's knowledge of transcendent being, and thereby the origin and meaning of mundane being, is constituted (75).

Voegelin stands firm on ground prepared by Plato, Aristotle, and St. Augustine against the imaginative manipulators of Second Realities of all persuasions. "The nature of a thing cannot be changed; whoever tries to 'alter' its nature destroys the thing. Man cannot transform himself into a superman; the attempt to create a superman is an attempt to murder man" (43). The Christian so-lution to the imperfection of the world remains open: ". . .the world throughout history will remain as it is and. . .man's salva-tional fulfillment is brought about through grace in death" (60). "The world. . .remains as it is given to us, and it is not within man's power to change its structure" (69). Thus More "in his revolt against the world as it has been created by God, arbitrarily omits an element of reality in order to create the fantasy of a new world" (70). "Hegel identifies his human logos with the Logos that is Christ, in order to make the meaningful process of history fully comprehensible. In the three cases of More, Hobbes, and Hegel,. . .the thinker suppresses an essential element of reality in order to be able to construct an image of man, or society, or history to suit his desires. . . . The constitution of being [however] remains what it is—beyond the reach of the thinker's lust for power. . . . The re-sult, therefore, is not dominion over being, but a fantasy satisfaction" (106).

Our materials all date from around 1960, and Voegelin meditated on these and related issues for another quarter-century before his death in 1985. The introduction to the 1974 volume of *Order and History,* the fourth volume, *The Ecumenic Age,* pursued the experiential analysis of Gnosticism in a meditation on the Beginning and the Beyond, which augmented and further solidified the theory as presented in his earlier work. This volume developed, in addition, an idea which supplemented the theory of rebellion and deformation in his earlier works, namely the important notion of "Egophanic revolt," the epiphany of the Ego, or the human Self experienced as autonomous, that lies at the core of the modern rebellion against the Ground of being. Moverover, the posthumously published volume of *Order and History,* volume five, *In Search of Order* (1987), alludes at several points to the problems of Gnosticism in a matter-of-fact way. As is evident in the present work, as well as in his later publications, Voegelin was constantly revising and refining his insights. As he commented in *Autobiographical Reflections,* whose material dates from 1973:

Since my first applications of Gnosticism to modern phenomena. . . , I have had to revise my position. The application of the category of Gnosticism to modern ideologies, of course, stands. In a more complete analysis, however, there are other factors to be considered in addition. One of these factors is the metastatic apocalypse deriving directly from the Israelite prophets, via Paul, and forming a permanent strand in Christian sectarian movements right up to the Renaissance. . . . I found, furthermore, that neither the apocalyptic nor the gnostic strand completely accounts for the process of immanentization. This factor has independent origins in the revival of neo-Platonism in Florence in the late fifteenth century.[4]

---

4. Eric Voegelin, *Autobiographical Reflections,* ed. Ellis Sandoz (1989; pb., Baton Rouge, 1996), 66-67. The passage continues in relevant comment.

A valuable subsequent statement came in a reported conversation in 1976 in which Voegelin replied to a question, in part as follows:

> I paid perhaps undue attention to gnosticism in the first book I published in English, *The New Science of Politics*. . . .I happened to run into the problem of gnosticism in my reading of Balthasar. But in the meanwhile we have found that the apocalyptic tradition is of equal importance, and the Neo-Platonic tradition, and hermeticism, and magic, and so on. [Still]. . .you will find that the gnostic mysticism of Ficino is a constant ever since the end of the fifteenth century, going on to the ideologies of the nineteenth century. So there are five or six such items—not only gnosticism—with which we have to deal.[5]

The power of Voegelin's analysis makes the work reprinted here both a pleasure to read and an illumination of superior order. But we must remember that his theory of Gnosticism is merely one facet of a great thinker's philosophy of history and human affairs. This book must be read, therefore, as part of Voegelin's valiant overall attempt to recover the truth of reality in an age of rebellion and unprecedented destruction.

Ellis Sandoz
Louisiana State University

5. *Conversations with Eric Voegelin,* ed. R. Eric O'Connor, Thomas More Institute Papers /76 (Montreal, 1980), 149. For a good survey and analysis of the other pertinent factors see David Walsh, *After Ideology: Recovering the Spiritual Foundations of Freedom* (1990; repr. Washington, D.C., 1995), 99-135, and the literature cited therein. The influence of the Gnosticism thesis is far greater than is commonly assumed. It can be seen without direct mention of Voegelin, for instance, in such disparate works as political scientist Zbigniew Brzezinski's *Out of Control* (New York, 1993); the best-seller by Harold Bloom, *Omens of Millennium: The Gnosis of Angels, Dreams, and Resurrection* (New York, 1996); and the technical study by Nathaniel Deutsch, *The Gnostic Imagination: Gnosticism, Mandaeism and Merkabah Mysticism* (Leiden, 1995).

FOREWORD TO THE AMERICAN EDITION

THE MORE WE come to know about the gnosis of antiquity, the more it becomes certain that modern movements of thought, such as progressivism, positivism, Hegelianism, and Marxism, are variants of gnosticism. The continuous interest in this problem goes back to the 1930's, when Hans Jonas published his first volume of *Gnosis und Spätantiker Geist* on ancient gnosis and Hans Urs von Balthasar his *Prometheus* on modern gnosticism. Their work was followed by more comprehensive studies of eighteenth- and nineteenth-century movements, such as Henri de Lubac's *Drame de l'Humanisme Athée* and Albert Camus's *L'Homme Révolté*. The lecture on "Science, Politics and Gnosticism," delivered in 1958 at the University of Munich, was an attempt to apply to the gnosticism of Hegel, Marx, Nietzsche, and Heidegger the insights gained by these predecessors, as well as by my own *New Science of Politics,* and to draw more clearly the lines that separate political gnosticism from a philosophy of politics. For the publication of this lecture the Introduction on the nature of gnosis and the section on "The Murder of God" were added. The essay "Ersatz Religion" was first published in *Wort und Wahrheit* (Vienna, 1960) in the interest of presenting to the general public a further elucidation of the symbolism and psychology of the mass movements of our time.

In America, the gnostic nature of the movements mentioned had been recognized early in the twentieth century by William James. He knew Hegel's speculation to be the culmination of modern gnosticism. The philosopher's critical opposition, however, had little effect; today, various intellectual movements of the gnostic type dominate the public scene in America no less than in Europe.

A representative case of the resultant intellectual confusion may be found in the "God is dead" movement. The death of God is the cardinal issue of gnosis, both ancient and modern. From Hegel to Nietzsche it is the great theme of gnostic speculation, and Protestant theology has been plagued by it ever since Hegel's time. In recent years, it has been taken up by American theologians who are faced with the pressing phenomena of urbanization and alienation. The attempt to come to grips with the problems of personal and social order when it is disrupted by gnosticisms, however, has not been very successful, because the philosophical knowledge that would be required for the purpose has itself been destroyed by the prevailing intellectual climate. The struggle against the consequences of gnosticism is being conducted in the very language of gnosticism. In this confused situation, the present essays will perhaps help us understand more clearly certain points currently under debate.

In the present state of science, a study of modern gnosticism is inevitably work in progress. Still, I find nothing to retract or correct, though a good deal would have to be added after the lapse of a decade, especially with regard to the problem of alienation. The reader who is interested in the subject of alienation might refer to my recent article "Immortality: Experience and Symbol" in the *Harvard Theological Review,* LX (July 1967), 235–79.

There remains the pleasant obligation to thank William J. Fitzpatrick for translating the first lecture and Gregor Sebba for his kind assistance.

Eric Voegelin
Ann Arbor, Michigan

PART ONE

Science, Politics and Gnosticism

I

INTRODUCTION

THE READER MAY well be surprised to see modern political thinkers and movements treated under the heading of "gnosticism." Since the state of science in this area is as yet largely unknown to the general public, an introductory explanation will not be unwelcome.

The idea that one of the main currents of European, especially of German, thought is essentially gnostic sounds strange today, but this is not a recent discovery. Until about a hundred years ago the facts of the matter were well known. In 1835 appeared Ferdinand Christian Baur's monumental work *Die christliche Gnosis, oder die Religionsphilosophie in ihrer geschichtlichen Entwicklung*. Under the heading "Ancient Gnosticism and Modern Philosophy of Religion," the last part of this work discusses: (1) Böhme's theosophy, (2) Schelling's philosophy of nature, (3) Schleiermacher's doctrine of faith, and (4) Hegel's philosophy of religion. The speculation of German idealism is correctly placed in its context in the gnostic movement since antiquity. Moreover, Baur's work was not an isolated event: it concluded a hundred years of preoccupation with the history of heresy—a branch of scholarship that not without reason developed during the Enlightenment. I shall mention only Johann Lorenz von Mosheim's encyclopedic *Versuch einer unparteiischen und gründlichen Ketzergeschichte* (Second Edition, 1748) and two works on ancient gnosticism from Baur's own day, Johann August Neander's *Genetische Entwicklung der vornehmsten gnostischen Systeme* (1818) and Jacques Matter's *Histoire critique du Gnosticisme et de son influence sur les sectes religieuses et philosophiques des six premiers siècles de l'ère chrétienne* (1828). It was well understood that with the Enlightenment and German idealism the gnostic movement had acquired great social significance.

On this issue as on many others, the learning and self-understanding of Western civilization were not submerged until the liberal era, the latter half of the nineteenth century, during the reign of positivism in the sciences of man and society. The submergence was so profound that when the gnostic movement reached its revolutionary phase its nature could no longer be recognized. The movements deriving from Marx and Bakunin, the early activities of Lenin, Sorel's myth of violence, the intellectual movement of neo-positivism, the communist, fascist, and national-socialist revolutions—all fell in a period, now fortunately part of the past, when science was at a low point. Europe had no conceptual tools with which to grasp the horror that was upon her. There was a scholarly study of the Christian churches and sects; there was a science of government, cast in the categories of the sovereign nation-state and its institutions; there were the beginnings of a sociology of power and political authority; but there was no science of the non-Christian, non-national intellectual and mass movements into which the Europe of Christian nation-states was in the process of breaking up. Since in its massiveness this new political phenomenon could not be disregarded, a number of stopgap notions were coined to cope with it. There was talk of neopagan movements, of new social and political myths, or of *mystiques politiques*. I, too, tried one of these ad hoc explanations in a little book on "political religions."

The confused state of science and the consequent impossibility of adequately understanding political phenomena lasted until well into the period of World War II. And for the general public this unfortunate situation still continues—otherwise, this preface would not be necessary. However, science has been undergoing a transformation, the beginnings of which go back some two generations. The recent catastrophes, which were centuries in the making, have not retarded, but accelerated it. And considering the extent of this change and the results already achieved, one can say that we are living in one of the great epochs of Western science. To be sure, the corruption persists; but if it does not lead to further catastrophes that put an end to the free existence of Western society, future historians may well date the spiritual and intellectual regeneration of the West from this flowering of science.

This is not the place, however, to go into the background and ramifications of this fascinating development. I can give only the briefest suggestion of recent scholarly work on ancient gnosticism and on the political expression of modern gnosticism.

The research on ancient gnosticism has a complex history of more than two hundred years. For this development one should consult the historical surveys in Wilhelm Bousset's *Die Hauptprobleme der Gnosis* (1907) and Hans Jonas's *Gnosis und spätantiker Geist* (1934; 1954). For the problems of gnosticism itself, see both these works and *Die Gnosis* (1924; Fourth Edition, 1955) by Hans Leisegang. Gilles Quispel's *Gnosis als Weltreligion* (1951) is a concise introduction by one of the foremost authorities.[1]

Under the influence of a deepened understanding of gnosticism and its connections with Judaism and Christianity, a new interpretation of European intellectual history and of modern politics has been developing. For example, Hans Urs von Balthasar's *Apokalypse der deutschen Seele* (1937), the first volume of which was reissued in 1947 under the title *Prometheus,* helps to clarify German history since the eighteenth century. The parallel work on French history is *L'Homme Révolté* (1951) by Albert Camus. And the interpretation of intellectual history that forms the basis for my present essay has moreover been strongly influenced by Henri de Lubac's *Drame de l'Humanisme Athée* (Second Edition, 1945) [*The Drama of*

---

1. Since the original German presentation of this essay, there has appeared a valuable comprehensive introduction to the whole subject by Hans Jonas, *The Gnostic Religion* (Boston, 1958), 2nd ed. (Boston, 1963).

Atheist Humanism, trans. Edith M. Riley (1950)]. Jakob Taubes' *Abendländische Eschatologie* (1947) is important for reestablishing the historical continuity of gnosticism from antiquity through the Middle Ages down to the political movements of modern times. Indispensable to any attempt to understand political sectarianism from the eleventh to the sixteenth century is the extensive presentation of material in Norman Cohn's *The Pursuit of the Millennium* (1957; Second Edition, 1961). Finally, my own studies on modern political gnosticism may be found in *The New Science of Politics* (1952).

And now a word on gnosticism itself—its origins and some of its essential characteristics.

For the cosmological civilizations of Mesopotamia, Syria, and Egypt, as well as for the peoples of the Mediterranean, the seventh century before Christ inaugurates the age of ecumenical empires. The Persian Empire is followed by the conquests of Alexander, the Diadochian empires, the expansion of the Roman Empire, and the creation of the Parthian and Sassanian empires. The collapse of the ancient empires of the East, the loss of independence for Israel and the Hellenic and Phoenician city-states, the population shifts, the deportations and enslavements, and the interpenetration of cultures reduce men who exercise no control over the proceedings of history to an extreme state of forlornness in the turmoil of the world, of intellectual disorientation, of material and spiritual insecurity. The loss of meaning that results from the breakdown of institutions, civilizations, and ethnic cohesion evokes attempts to regain an understanding of the meaning of human existence in the given conditions of the world. Among these efforts, which vary widely in depth of insight and substantive truth, are to be found: the Stoic reinterpretation of man (to whom the polis had become meaningless) as the *polites* (citizen) of the cosmos, the Polybian vision of a pragmatic ecumene destined to be created by Rome, the mystery religions, the Heliopolitan slave cults, Hebrew apocalyptic, Christianity, and Manichaeism.

And in this sequence, as one of the most grandiose of the new formulations of the meaning of existence, belongs gnosticism.

Of the profusion of gnostic experiences and symbolic expressions, one feature may be singled out as the central element in this varied and extensive creation of meaning: the experience of the world as an alien place into which man has strayed and from which he must find his way back home to the other world of his origin. "Who has cast me into the suffering of this world?" asks the "Great Life" of the gnostic texts, which is also the "first, alien Life from the worlds of light."[2] It is an alien in this world and this world is alien to it.

"This world was not made according to the desire of the Life." "Not by the will of the Great Life art thou come hither." Therefore the question, "Who conveyed me into the evil darkness?" and the entreaty, "Deliver us from the darkness of this world into which we are flung." The world is no longer the well-ordered, the cosmos, in which Hellenic man felt at home; nor is it the Judaeo-Christian world that God created and found good. Gnostic man no longer wishes to perceive in admiration the intrinsic order of the cosmos. For him the world has become a prison from which he wants to escape: "The wretched soul has strayed into a labyrinth of torment and wanders around without a way out. . . . It seeks to escape from the bitter chaos, but knows not how to get out." Therefore the confused, plaintive question asked of the Great Life, "Why didst thou create this world, why didst thou order the tribes here from thy midst?" From this attitude springs the programmatic formula of gnosticism, which Clement of Alexandria recorded: Gnosis is "the knowledge of who we were and what we became, of where we were and whereinto we have been flung, of whereto we are hastening and wherefrom we are redeemed, of what birth is and what rebirth." The great speculative mythopoems of gnosticism revolve

---

2. Discussions of these and the following texts can be found in Hans Jonas, *The Gnostic Religion*.

around the questions of origin, the condition of having-been-flung, escape from the world, and the means of deliverance.

In the quoted texts the reader will have recognized Hegel's alienated spirit and Heidegger's flungness (*Geworfenheit*) of human existence. This similarity in symbolic expression results from a homogeneity in experience of the world. And the homogeneity goes beyond the experience of the world to the image of man and salvation with which both the modern and the ancient gnostics respond to the condition of "flungness" in the alien world.

If man is to be delivered from the world, the possibility of deliverance must first be established in the order of being. In the ontology of ancient gnosticism this is accomplished through faith in the "alien," "hidden" God who comes to man's aid, sends him his messengers, and shows him the way out of the prison of the evil God of this world (be he Zeus or Yahweh or one of the other ancient father gods). In modern gnosticism it is accomplished through the assumption of an absolute spirit which in the dialectical unfolding of consciousness proceeds from alienation to consciousness of itself; or through the assumption of a dialectical-material process of nature which in its course leads from the alienation resulting from private property and belief in God to the freedom of a fully human existence; or through the assumption of a will of nature which transforms man into superman.

Within the ontic possibility, however, gnostic man must carry on the work of salvation himself. Now, through his psyche ("soul") he belongs to the order, the *nomos,* of the world; what impels him toward deliverance is the pneuma ("spirit"). The labor of salvation, therefore, entails the dissolution of the worldly constitution of the psyche and at the same time the gathering and freeing of the powers of the pneuma. However the phases of salvation are represented in the different sects and systems—and they vary from magic practices to mystic ecstasies, from libertinism through indifferentism to the world to the strictest asceticism—the aim always is destruction of the old world and passage to the new. The instrument of salvation is gnosis itself—knowledge. Since according to the gnostic ontology entanglement with the world is brought about by *agnoia,* ignorance, the soul will be able to disentangle itself through knowledge of its true life and its condition of alienness in this world. As the knowledge of falling captive to the world, gnosis is at the same time the means of escaping it. Thus, Irenaeus recounts the meaning that gnosis had for the Valentinians:

> Perfect salvation consists in the cognition, as such, of the Ineffable Greatness. For since sin and affliction resulted from ignorance *(agnoia),* this whole system originating in ignorance is dissolved through knowledge *(gnosis).* Hence, gnosis is the salvation of the inner man. . . . Gnosis redeems the inner, pneumatic man; he finds his satisfaction in the knowledge of the Whole. And this is the true salvation.

This will have to suffice by way of clarification, save for one word of caution. Self-salvation through knowledge has its own magic, and this magic is not harmless. The structure of the order of being will not change because one finds it defective and runs away from it. The attempt at world destruction will not destroy the world, but will only increase the disorder in society. The gnostic's flight from a truly dreadful, confusing, and oppressive state of the world is understandable. But the order of the ancient world was renewed by that movement which strove through loving action to revive the practice of the "serious play" (to use Plato's expression)—that is, by Christianity.

II

SCIENCE, POLITICS AND GNOSTICISM

I

POLITICAL SCIENCE, *politike episteme,* was founded by Plato and Aristotle.

At stake in the spiritual confusion of the time was whether there could be fashioned an image of the right order of the soul and society—a paradigm, a model, an ideal—that could function for the citizens of the polis as had paraenetic myth for the Homeric heroes. To be sure, fourth-century Athens afforded plenty of opinions about the right manner of living and the right order of society. But was it possible to show that one of the multitude of sceptic, hedonist, utilitarian, power oriented, and partisan *doxai* was the true one? Or, if none of them could stand up to critical examination, could a new image of order be formed that would not also bear the marks of a non-binding, subjective opinion *(doxa)*? The science of political philosophy resulted from the efforts to find an answer to this question.

In its essentials the classical foundation of political science is still valid today. We shall outline briefly its subject matter, analytical method, and anthropological presuppositions.

As for the subject matter, it is nothing esoteric; rather, it lies not far from the questions of the day and is concerned with the truth of things that everyone talks about. What is happiness? How should a man live in order to be happy? What is virtue? What, especially, is the virtue of justice? How large a territory and a population are best for a society? What kind of education is best? What professions, and what form of government? All of these questions arise from the conditions of the existence of man in society. And the philosopher is a man like any other: as far as the order of society is concerned, he has no other questions to ask than those of his fellow citizens.

However, his questioning leads to a conflict with opinion. This is quite another kind of conflict than that between differing opinions; for although the philosopher's questions are concerned with the same subjects as those of the philodoxer (these are the terms Plato adopted to describe the adversaries), the nature of his inquiry is radically different. The philosopher's question represents an attempt to advance beyond opinion to truth through the use of scientific analysis as developed by Aristotle in the *Analytica Posteriora*. With the instrument of analysis current statements about political matters are broken down into pre-analytic opinions and scientific propositions in the strict sense; and the verbal symbols, into pre-analytic or insufficiently analyzed expressions and the analytic concepts of political science. In this way, advocates of opinions who attack one another in daily politics are grouped together over against their common adversary, the philosopher.

When we speak of scientific analysis, we wish to emphasize the contrast with formal analysis. An analysis by means of formal logic can lead to no more than a demonstration that an opinion suffers from an inherent contradiction, or that different opinions contradict one another, or that conclusions have been invalidly drawn. A scientific analysis, on the other hand, makes it possible to judge of the truth of the premises implied by an opinion. It can do this, however, only on the assumption that truth about the order of being—to which, of course, opinions also refer—is objectively ascertainable. And Platonic-Aristotelian analysis does in fact operate on the assumption that there is an order of being accessible to a science beyond opinion. Its aim is knowledge of the order of being, of the levels of the hierarchy of being and their interrelationships, of the essential structure of the realms of being, and especially of human nature and its place in the totality of being. Analysis, therefore, is scientific and leads to a science of order through the fact that, and insofar as, it is ontologically oriented.

The assumption alone, however—that the order of being is accessible to knowledge, that ontology is possible—is still not enough to carry out an analysis; for the assumption might be unfounded. Therefore, an insight concerning being must always be really present—not only so that the first steps of the analysis can be taken, but so that the very idea of the analysis can be conceived and developed at all. And indeed, Platonic-Aristotelian analysis did not in the least begin with speculations about its own possibility, but with the actual insight into being which motivated the analytical process. The decisive event in the establishment of *politike episteme* was the specifically philosophical realization that the levels of being discernible within the world are surmounted by a transcendent source of being and its order. And this insight was itself rooted in the real movements of the human spiritual soul toward divine being experienced as transcendent. In the experiences of love for the world-transcendent origin of being, in *philia* toward the *sophon* (the wise), in *eros* toward the *agathon* (the good) and the *kalon* (the beautiful), man became philosopher. From these experiences arose the image of the order of being. At the opening of the soul—that is the metaphor Bergson uses to describe the event—the order of being becomes visible even to its ground and origin in the beyond, in the Platonic *epekeina,* in which the soul participates as it suffers and achieves its opening.

Only when the order of being as a whole, unto its origin in transcendent being, comes into view, can the analysis be undertaken with any hope of success; for only then can current opinions about right order be examined as to their agreement with the order of being. When the strong and successful are highly rated, they can then be contrasted with those who possess the virtue of *phronesis,* wisdom, who live *sub specie mortis* and act with the Last Judgment in mind. When statesmen are praised for having made their people great and powerful, as Themistocles and Pericles had made Athens, Plato can confront them with the moral decline that was the result of their policies. (One thinks here not only of classical examples, but perhaps also of what Gladstone said of Bismarck: He made Germany great and the Germans small.) Again: when impetuous young men are repelled by the vulgarity of democracy, Plato can point out to them that energy, pride, and will to rule can indeed establish the despotism of a spiritually corrupt elite, but not a just government; and when democrats rave about freedom and equality and forget that government requires spiritual training and intellectual discipline, he can warn them that they are on the way to tyranny.

These examples will suffice to indicate that political science goes beyond the validity of propositions to the truth of existence. The opinions for the clarification of which the analysis is undertaken are not merely false: they are symptoms of spiritual disorder in the men who hold them. And the purpose of the analysis is to persuade—to have its own insights, if possible, supplant the opinions in social reality. Analysis is concerned with the therapy of order.[3]

Society resists the therapeutic activity of science. Because not only the validity of the opinions is called into question but also the truth of the human attitudes expressed in the opinions, because the effort in behalf of truth is directed at the untruth of existence in particular men, the intellectual debate is intensified beyond the point of analysis and argument to that of existential struggle for and against truth— struggle that can be waged on every level of human existence, from spiritual persuasion, *peitho* in the Platonic sense, to psychological propaganda, to even physical attack and destruction. Today, under the pressure of totalitarian terror, we are perhaps inclined to think primarily of the physical forms of

---

3. On the problem of rational debate in a heavily ideologized society, see Eric Voegelin, "On Debate and Existence," *The Intercollegiate Review,* III (1967), 143–52.

opposition. But they are not the most successful. The opposition becomes truly radical and dangerous only when philosophical questioning is itself called into question, when *doxa* takes on the appearance of philosophy, when it arrogates to itself the name of science and prohibits science as nonscience. Only if this prohibition can be made socially effective will the point have been reached where *ratio* can no longer operate as a remedy for spiritual disorder. Hellenic civilization never came to this: philosophizing could be mortally dangerous, but philosophy, especially political science, flourished. Never did it occur to a Greek to prohibit analytical inquiry as such.

The frame of reference of political science has changed considerably in the more than two thousand years since its founding. The broadening of temporal and spatial horizons has yielded to comparative analysis enormous amounts of material that were unknown in antiquity. And the appearance of Christianity in history, with the resulting tension between reason and revelation, has profoundly affected the difficulties of philosophizing. The Platonic-Aristotelian paradigm of the best polis cannot provide an answer for the great questions of our time—either for the organizational problems of industrial society or for the spiritual problems of the struggle between Christianity and ideology. But the basic situation of political science, which I have briefly outlined here, has, except in one respect, not changed at all. Today, just as two thousand years ago, *politike episteme* deals with questions that concern everyone and that everyone asks. Though different opinions are current in society today, its subject matter has not changed. Its method is still scientific analysis. And the prerequisite of analysis is still the perception of the order of being unto its origin in transcendent being, in particular, the loving openness of the soul to its transcendent ground of order.

Only in one respect has the situation of political science changed. As indicated, there has emerged a phenomenon unknown to antiquity that permeates our modern societies so completely that its ubiquity scarcely leaves us any room to see it at all: the prohibition of questioning. This is not a matter of resistance to analysis—that existed in antiquity as well. It does not involve those who cling to opinions by reason of tradition or emotion, or those who engage in debate in a naive confidence in the rightness of their opinions and who take the offensive only when analysis unnerves them. Rather, we are confronted here with persons who know that, and why, their opinions cannot stand up under critical analysis and who therefore make the prohibition of the examination of their premises part of their dogma. This position of a conscious, deliberate, and painstakingly elaborated obstruction of *ratio* constitutes the new phenomenon.

II

We shall now try to present the phenomenon of the prohibition of questions through an analysis of representative opinions. Thus, this effort will present not only the phenomenon, but the exercise of analysis as well. It should show that the spiritual disorder of our time, the civilizational crisis of which everyone so readily speaks, does not by any means have to be borne as an inevitable fate; that, on the contrary, everyone possesses the means of overcoming it in his own life. And our effort should not only indicate the means, but also show how to employ them. No one is obliged to take part in the spiritual crisis of a society; on the contrary, everyone is obliged to avoid this folly and live his life in order. Our presentation of the phenomenon, therefore, will at the same time furnish the remedy for it through therapeutic analysis.

1

The prohibition of questions as it appears in some of the early writings of Karl Marx—the "Economic and Philosophical Manuscripts" of 1844—can serve as the point of departure.

Marx is a speculative gnostic. He construes the order of being as a process of nature complete in itself. Nature is in a state of becoming, and in the course of its development it has brought forth man: "*Man is directly a being of nature.*"⁴ Now, in the development of nature a special role has devolved upon man. This being, which is itself nature, also stands over against nature and assists it in its development by human labor—which in its highest form is technology and industry based on the natural sciences: "Nature as it develops in human history . . . as it develops through industry . . . is true *anthropological* nature."⁵ In the process of creating nature, however, man at the same time also creates himself to the fullness of his being; therefore, "*all of so-called world history* is nothing but the production of man by human labor."⁶ The purpose of this speculation is to shut off the process of being from transcendent being and have man create himself. This is accomplished by playing with equivocations in which "nature" is now all-inclusive being, now nature as opposed to man, and now the nature of man in the sense of *essentia*. This equivocal wordplay reaches its climax in a sentence that can easily be overlooked: "A being that does not have its nature outside of itself is not a *natural* being; it does not participate in the being of nature."⁷

In connection with this speculation Marx himself now brings up the question of what objection the "particular individual" would probably have to the idea of the spontaneous generation *("generatio aequivoca")* of nature and man: "The being-of-itself *(Durchsichselbstsein)* of nature and man is *inconceivable* to him, because it contradicts all the *tangible aspects* of practical life." The individual man will, going back from generation to generation in search of his

4. Karl Marx, *"Nationalökonomie und Philosophie,"* in Karl Marx, *Der Historische Materialismus: Die Frühschriften,* ed. Landshut and Meyer (Leipzig, 1932), p. 333 ["Economic and Philosophical Manuscripts," in *Early Writings,* ed. and trans. T. B. Bottomore (New York, 1964), p. 206].

5. *Ibid.,* p. 304 [Bottomore, p. 164].

6. *Ibid.,* p. 307 [Bottomore, p. 166].

7. *Ibid.,* p. 333 [Bottomore, p. 207].

origin, raise the question of the creation of the first man. He will introduce the argument of infinite regress, which in Ionian philosophy led to the problem of the *arche* (origin). To such questions, prompted by the "tangible" experience that man does not exist of himself, Marx chooses to reply that they are "a product of abstraction." "When you inquire about the creation of nature and man, you abstract from nature and man." Nature and man are real only as Marx construes them in his speculation. Should his questioner pose the possibility of their non-existence, then Marx could not prove that they exist.[8]

In reality, his construct would collapse with this question. And how does Marx get out of the predicament? He instructs his questioner, "Give up your abstraction and you will give up your question along with it." If the questioner were consistent, says Marx, he would have to think of himself as not existing—even while, in the very act of questioning, he *is*. Hence, again the instruction: "Do not think, do not question me."[9] The "individual man," however, is not obliged to be taken in by Marx's syllogism and think of himself as not existing because he is aware of the fact that he does not exist of himself. Indeed, Marx concedes this very point—without, however, choosing to go into it. Instead, he breaks off the debate by declaring that "for socialist man"—that is, for the man who has accepted Marx's construct of the process of being and history— such a question "becomes a practical impossibility." The questions of the "individual man" are cut off by the ukase of the speculator who will not permit his construct to be disturbed. When "socialist man" speaks, man has to be silent.[10]

This, then, is the evidence from which we have to proceed. But before we take up the analysis itself, let us first establish that the

8. *Ibid.,* pp. 306–307 [Bottomore, pp. 165–66].

9. *Ibid.,* p. 307 [Bottomore, p. 166].

10. *Ibid.* [Bottomore, pp. 166–67].

Marxian prohibition of questions is neither isolated nor harmless. It was not isolated in its own time, for we find the same prohibition in Comte, in the first Lecture of his *Cours de Philosophie Positive*. Comte also anticipates objections to his construct, and he bluntly dismisses them as idle questions. For the present he is interested only in the laws of social phenomena. Whoever asks questions about the nature, calling, and destiny of man may be temporarily ignored; later, after the system of positivism has prevailed in society, such persons will have to be silenced by appropriate measures.[11] And the prohibition of questions is not harmless, for it has attained great social effectiveness among men who forbid themselves to ask questions in critical situations. One thinks of the observation of Rudolf Höss, the commandant of the extermination camp at Auschwitz. When asked why he did not refuse to obey the order to organize the mass executions, he replied: "At that time I did not indulge in deliberation: I had received the order, and I had to carry it out. . . . I do not believe that even one of the thousands of SS leaders could have permitted such a thought to occur to him. Something like that was just completely impossible."[12] This is very close to the wording of Marx's declaration that for "socialist man" such a question "becomes a practical impossibility." Thus, we see delineated three major types for whom a human inquiry has become a practical impossibility: socialist man (in the Marxian sense), positivist man (in the Comtean sense), and national-socialist man.

And now for the Marxian suppression of questions. It represents, as we shall see, a very complicated psychological phenomenon, and we must isolate each of its components in turn. First, the most "tangible": here is a thinker who knows that his construct will collapse

11. Auguste Comte, *Cours de Philosophie Positive*, I (Paris, 1830).

12. Rudolf Höss, *Kommandant in Auschwitz*, as quoted in the *Süddeutsche Zeitung*, 1 October 1958.

as soon as the basic philosophical question is asked. Does this knowledge induce him to abandon his untenable construct? Not in the least: it merely induces him to prohibit such questions. But his prohibition now induces us to ask, Was Marx an intellectual swindler? Such a question will perhaps give rise to objections. Can one seriously entertain the idea that the lifework of a thinker of considerable rank is based on an intellectual swindle? Could it have attracted a mass following and become a political world power if it rested on a swindle? But we today are inured to such scruples: we have seen too many improbable and incredible things that were nonetheless real. Therefore, we hesitate neither to ask the question that the evidence presses upon us, nor to answer, Yes, Marx *was* an intellectual swindler. This is certainly not the last word on Marx. We have already referred to the complexity of the psychological phenomenon behind the passages quoted. But it must unrelentingly be the first word if we do not want to obstruct our understanding of the prohibition of questions.

When we establish that Marx was an intellectual swindler, the further question of why immediately arises. What can prompt a man to commit such a swindle? Is there not something pathological about this act? For an answer to this question let us turn to Nietzsche, who was also a speculative gnostic, but a more sensitive psychologist than Marx.

2

Nietzsche introduces the will to power, the will to dominion, the *libido dominandi,* as the passion that accounts for the will to intellectual deception. Let us examine the *via dolorosa* along which this passion drives the gnostic thinker from one station to the next.

In *Jenseits von Gut und Böse,* Aphorism 230, Nietzsche speaks of a "fundamental will of the spirit" which wants to feel itself master. The spirit's will to mastery is served in the first place by "a suddenly erupt-ing resolve for ignorance, for arbitrary occlusion . . . a kind of defensive stand against much that is knowable." Moreover, the spirit *wills* to let itself be deceived on occasion, "perhaps with a mis-chievous suspicion that things are *not* thus and so, but rather only al-lowed to pass as such . . . a satisfaction in the arbitrariness of all these manifestations of power." Finally, there belongs here "that not un-scrupulous readiness of the spirit to deceive other spirits and to dis-semble before them," the enjoyment of "cunning and a variety of masks."[13]

The *libido dominandi*, however, has a violence and cruelty that go beyond the delight in masquerade and in the deception of others. It turns on the thinker himself and unmasks his thought as a cunning will to power. "A kind of cruelty of the intellectual conscience," "an extravagant honesty," clears up the deception; however—and this is the decisive point—not in order to advance to the truth beyond the deception, but only to set up a new one in place of the old. The game of masks continues; and those who allow themselves to be deceived remain deceived. In this "cruelty of the intellectual conscience" can be seen the movement of the spirit that in Nietzsche's gnosis corre-sponds functionally to the Platonic *periagoge*, the turning-around and opening of the soul. But in the gnostic movement man remains shut off from transcendent being. The will to power strikes against the wall of being, which has become a prison. It forces the spirit into the rhythm of deception and self-laceration.[14]

The compulsion to deceive must now be examined further. Does the spirit really strike against the wall of being? Or does it not perhaps *will* to stop there? The remoter depths of the will to power are revealed through the following aphorism: "To rule, and

13. Nietzsche, No. 230, *Jenseits von Gut und Böse,* in *Werke,* VII (Leipzig, 1903), pp. 187–88 [*Beyond Good and Evil,* trans. Marianne Cowan (Chicago, 1955), pp. 158–59].

14. *Ibid.,* p. 189 [Cowan, p. 160].

to be no longer a servant of a god: this means was left behind to ennoble man." To rule means to be God; in order to be God gnostic man takes upon himself the torments of deception and self-laceration.[15]

But the spirit's action is not yet at an end. The question of whether the thinker really wants to be God takes us still further; perhaps the affirmation of this desire is just another deception. In the "Night Song" in *Zarathustra* this question is answered in a revealing confession:

> It is night: only now awaken all the songs of the lovers. . . . A craving for love is in me. . . . [But] light am I: oh, that I were night! . . . This is my loneliness, that I am begirt with light. . . . I do not know the happiness of those who receive. . . . This is my poverty, that my hand never rests from giving. . . . You only, you dark ones, you of the night, extract your warmth from what shines. . . . Ice is around me; my hand is burnt up with iciness. . . . It is night: alas, that I must be light.

In this confession the voice of a spiritually sensitive man seems to be speaking, who is suffering in the consciousness of his demonic occlusion. Mystic night is denied him. He is imprisoned in the icy light of his existence. And from this prison rises the protestation—half lament, half prayer, and still not free of the defiance of the rebel— "And my soul, too, is the song of a lover."[16]

No one will hear this lament of a man to whom humility before God was not given without being moved. Beyond the psychology of the will to power, we are confronted with the inscrutable fact that grace is granted or denied.

15. Nietzsche, No. 250, *Sprüche und Sentenzen* (1882–1884), in *Werke*, XII (Leipzig, 1901), 282.
16. Nietzsche, "Night Song," *Also sprach Zarathustra*, in *Werke*, VI (Leipzig, 1904), 153–55 [*Thus Spoke Zarathusra*, trans. Marianne Cowan (Chicago, 1957), pp. 106–108].

Yet emotion should not prevent our seeing the dubiousness of this confession. We introduced it by asking whether the gnostic thinker really wants to be God, or whether the affirmation of his will is not just another deception. The "Night Song" appears to admit the deception: it is not that he *wants* to be God; he *has* to be God—for inscrutable reasons. But this latter conclusion, which nullifies the former one, immediately prompts us to ask if we have to accept it. Must we now consider the game of deceptions ended? I do not think so. Let us continue with the game and ask if the "Night Song" is not yet another mask. Bearing in mind that Nietzsche confesses that he knows his occlusion and suffers in it, let us turn his confession against him and ask, Does a man really have to make a virtue out of the misery of his condition, which he perceives to be the graceless disorder of the soul, and set it up as a superhuman ideal? Does his deficiency entitle him to perform Dionysian dances with masks? Let us, with the brutality that the times compel if we are not to fall victim to them, ask if he is not rather obliged to be silent. And if his lament were more than a mask, if it were genuine, if he suffered from his condition, would he not then be speechless? But Nietzsche is not in the least speechless; and his eloquence is convincing proof that the lament is only an act of sympathetic understanding, that it has not been allowed to touch the core of his existence in rebellion against God, and therefore that it is not genuine, but a mask. Just as Marx will not permit his game of equivocations to be disturbed, so Nietzsche refuses to break off his game of masks.

The phenomenon of the prohibition of questions is becoming clearer in its outlines. The gnostic thinker really does commit an intellectual swindle, and he knows it. One can distinguish three stages in the action of his spirit. On the surface lies the deception itself. It could be self-deception; and very often it is, when the speculation of a creative thinker has culturally degenerated and become the dogma of a mass movement. But when the phenomenon is apprehended at its point of origin, as in Marx or Nietzsche, deeper than the deception itself will be found the awareness of it. The thinker does not lose control of himself: the *libido dominandi* turns on its own work and wishes to master the deception as well. This gnostic turning back on itself corresponds spiritually, as we have said, to the philosophic conversion, the *periagoge* in the Platonic sense. However, the gnostic movement of the spirit does not lead to the erotic opening of the soul, but rather to the deepest reach of persistence in the deception, where revolt against God is revealed to be its motive and purpose.

With the three stages in the spirit's action it is now possible also to differentiate more precisely the corresponding levels of deception:

1) For the surface act it will be convenient to retain the term Nietzsche used, "deception." But in content this action does not necessarily differ from a wrong judgment arising from another motive than the gnostic. It could also be an "error." It becomes a deception only because of the psychological context.

2) In the second stage the thinker becomes aware of the untruth of his assertion or speculation, but persists in it in spite of this knowledge. Only because of his awareness of the untruth does the action become a deception. And because of the persistence in the communication of what are recognized to be false arguments, it also becomes an "intellectual swindle."

3) In the third stage the revolt against God is revealed and recognized to be the motive of the swindle. With the continuation of the intellectual swindle in full knowledge of the motive of revolt the deception further becomes "demonic mendacity."

3

The first and second of the three stages Nietzsche described can be seen in the texts that we have quoted from Marx. How does Marx stand with respect to the third stage in this movement of the spirit, where rebellion against God is revealed to be the motive for the deception? This is exactly what is revealed in the context of the quoted passages:

A *being* regards itself as independent only when it stands on its own feet; and it stands on its feet only when it owes its *existence* to itself alone. A man who lives by the grace of another considers himself a dependent being. But I live by the grace of another completely if I owe him not only the maintenance of my life but also *its creation:* if he is the *source* of my life; and my life necessarily has such a cause outside itself if it is not my own creation.[17]

Marx does not deny that "tangible experience" argues for the dependence of man. But reality must be destroyed—this is the great concern of gnosis. In its place steps the gnostic who produces the independence of his existence by speculation. It would indeed be difficult to find another passage in gnostic literature that so clearly exposes this speculation as an attempt to replace the reality of being with a "second reality" (as Robert Musil called this undertaking).

A passage from Marx's doctoral dissertation of 1840–41 takes us still further into the problem of revolt:

Philosophy makes no secret of it. The confession of Prometheus, "In a word, I hate all the gods," is its own confession, its own verdict against all gods heavenly and earthly who do not acknowledge human self-consciousness as the supreme deity. There shall be none beside it.[18]

In this confession, in which the young Marx presents his own attitude under the symbol of Prometheus, the vast history of the

---

17. Marx, *"Nationalökonomie und Philosophie,"* pp. 305–306 [Bottomore, p. 165].

18. Marx, *Differenz der demokritischen und epikurischen Naturphilosophie nebst einem Anhang,* in Karl Marx and Friedrich Engels, *Historisch-Kritische Gesamtausgabe,* Part I, I/1 (Frankfurt, 1927), 10. The dissertation was written in 1839–41; the preface was dated: Berlin, March 1841. ["Foreword to Thesis: *The Difference Between the Natural Philosophy of Democritus and the Natural Philosophy of Epicurus,"* in Karl Marx and Friedrich Engels, *On Religion* (New York, 1964), p. 15].

revolt against God is illuminated as far back as the Hellenic creation of the symbol.

Let us first clarify the relationship between Marx's comments and the verse he quotes from Aeschylus.

Prometheus is riveted to a rock by the sea. Below on the strip of beach stands Hermes looking up at him. The fettered Prometheus gives his bitterness free reign. Hermes tries to calm him and urges moderation. Then, Prometheus crams his impotence and rebellion into the line quoted by Marx: "In a word, I hate all the gods."[19] But the line is not part of a monologue. At this outbreak of hatred the messenger of the gods replies admonishingly: "It appears you have been stricken with no small madness."[20] The word translated here as "madness" is the Greek *nosos* which Aeschylus employed as a synonym for *nosema*.[21] It means bodily or mental sickness. In the sense of a disease of the spirit it can mean hatred of the gods or simply being dominated by one's passions. For example, Plato speaks of the *nosema tes adikias,* the sickness of injustice.[22] Here we touch on the diseased—the pneumopathological—nature of the revolt that was pointed out earlier. And what does Marx say to this observation of the messenger of the gods? He says nothing. Anyone who does not know *Prometheus Bound* must conclude that the quoted "confession" sums up the meaning of the tragedy, not that Aeschylus wished to represent hatred of the gods as madness. In the distortion of the intended meaning into its opposite the suppression of questions can be seen again on all its levels: the deception of the reader by isolating the text (the confession appears in the preface to a doctoral dissertation), the awareness of the swindle (for we assume that Marx had read the tragedy), and the demonic persistence in the revolt against better judgment.

19. Aeschylus, *Prometheus Bound,* 975.
20. *Ibid.,* 977.
21. *Ibid.,* 978.
22. Plato, *Gorgias,* 480b.

The soul's rebellion against the order of the cosmos, hatred of the gods, and the revolt of the Titans are not, to be sure, unheard of in Hellenic myth. But the Titanomachia ends with the victory of Jovian justice *(dike)*, and Prometheus is fettered. The revolutionary reversal of the symbol—the dethronement of the gods, the victory of Prometheus—lies beyond classical culture; it is the work of gnosticism. Not until the gnostic revolt of the Roman era do Prometheus, Cain, Eve, and the serpent become symbols of man's deliverance from the power of the tyrannical god of this world. Marx's confession iterates the reinterpretation of the Prometheus symbol that can be found in an alchemist text of the third century, the treatise of Zosimos *On the Letter Omega*:

> Hermes and Zoroaster have said that the tribe of philosophers is above fate *(heimarmene)*: they do not rejoice in the good fortune it brings, for they master their desires; nor are they affected by the bad fortune it sends—if it is true that they look ahead to the end of all their misfortune; nor do they accept the fine gifts that come from it, for they pass their lives in immateriality. This is the point of Prometheus' advice to Epimetheus in Hesiod:
>
> [PROMETHEUS.] What in the eyes of men is the greatest good fortune?
> [EPIMETHEUS.]   A beautiful woman and lots of money.
> [PROMETHEUS.] Beware of accepting gifts from Olympian Zeus; put them far from you.

In this way, he teaches his brother to reject the gifts of Zeus, i.e., of heimarmene, through the power of philosophy.[23]

---

23. *Collection des Anciens Alchemistes Grecs,* ed. Berthelot (Paris, 1888), III, 228ff. (Greek text), 221ff. (translation). Our translation follows that of Festugière, together with his emendations: A. J. Festugière, *La Révélation d'Hermès Trismégiste, Vol. I: L'Astrologie et les Sciences Occultes,* 2nd ed. (Paris, 1950), p. 266. For Prometheus' answer in Hesiod, see *Works and Days,* 85–87.

This text has a special significance for us, because it confirms the connection between the revolt against the gods and the proclamation of "philosophy" as the new source of order and authority. Not only does Prometheus become the hero of revolution, the symbol of philosophy undergoes a similar perversion of its meaning. The "philosophy" of Zosimos is not the philosophy that Plato founded. His "philosophers" are not, as in the Platonic myth, the Sons of Zeus who follow his lead in this world and the next; nor are they the priests and helpers of the gods, as in Marcus Aurelius; their efforts are not concerned with forming men for the order of Zeus and *dike*. And "philosophizing" is not the Socratic practice of dying so that a man may measure up at the Last Judgment. The "philosophy" of Zosimos is concerned with something else, although the text, to the extent quoted, does not sufficiently make clear with what. Certainly, it is concerned with a new asceticism, with the attempt to remove oneself from the world and its entanglements—the gnostic motive of doing away with reality. (The transformation of Pandora and her gifts into "a beautiful woman and lots of money" carries overtones of antibourgeois criticism.) Certainly, it has to do with a revolt against the father-gods of classical myth, for the identification of the gifts of Zeus with the dispensations of what by Zosimos' time was a thoroughly discredited *heimarmene* is doubtless intended disparagingly. Certainly, it is involved in an *opus* of delivering man from the evil of the world. And finally, it is certain that "philosophy" is, in some way or other, intended as an instrument of salvation available for man's use.[24]

Whether Marx knew this text either directly or indirectly, we cannot say. Probably he did not. All the more, then, would the

---

24. For the Prometheus symbolism in Zosimos, see Hans Jonas, *Gnosis und spätantiker Geist,* Vol. I: Die mythologische Gnosis (Göttingen, 1954), pp. 218–20; for the revolutionary element in gnosticism, see the entire section, pp. 214–51. There is also a brief discussion in Jonas, *The Gnostic Religion,* pp. 91–97.

parallel in symbolic expression corroborate the essential sameness of attitudes and motives in ancient and modern gnosticism.[25]

4

Now just what is this new "philosophy"? What is its connection with the Promethian revolt and with the suppression of questions? Marx modelled his idea of science and philosophy on Hegel. Let us turn, therefore, to the greatest of speculative gnostics for the answer to these questions.

It is to be found in a fundamental statement in the Preface to the *Phänomenologie* of 1807:

The true form in which truth exists can only be the scientific system of it. To contribute to bringing philosophy closer to the form of science—the goal of being able to cast off the name love of *knowledge (Liebe zum Wissen)* and become *actual knowledge (wirkliches Wissen)*—is the task I have set for myself.[26]

The expressions "love of knowledge" and "actual knowledge" are italicized by Hegel himself. If we translate them back into the Greek, into *philosophia* and *gnosis,* we then have before us the program of advancing from philosophy to gnosis. Thus, Hegel's programmatic formula implies the perversion of the symbols science and philosophy.

25. The Prometheus complex in Marx can be fully understood only when seen in the context of German idealism. For the relevant historical background, see Hans Urs von Balthasar's masterly work *Prometheus: Studien zur Geschichte des deutschen Idealismus,* 2nd ed. (Heidelberg, 1947). Unfortunately the book contains no study of Marx. See also Eric Voegelin, "The Formation of the Marxian Revolutionary Idea," *Review of Politics,* XII (1950), 275–302.

26. Hegel, *Phänomenologie des Geistes,* ed. Johannes Hoffmeister (Hamburg, 1952), p. 12 [*The Phenomenology of Mind,* trans. J. B. Baillie, 2nd ed., revised (London, 1949), p. 70].

By philosophy Hegel means an undertaking of thought that approaches and can finally attain actual knowledge. Philosophy is subsumed under the idea of progress in the eighteenth-century sense of the term. As opposed to this progressivist idea of philosophy let us recall Plato's efforts to clarify its nature. In the *Phaedrus* Plato has Socrates describe the characteristics of the true thinker. When Phaedrus asks what one should call such a man, Socrates, following Heraclitus, replies that the term *sophos,* one who knows, would be excessive: this attribute may be applied to God alone; but one might well call him *philosophos.*[27] Thus, "actual knowledge" is reserved to God; finite man can only be the "lover of knowledge," not himself the one who knows. In the meaning of the passage, the lover of the knowledge that belongs only to the knowing God, the *philosophos,* becomes the *theophilos,* the lover of God. If we now place Hegel's idea of philosophizing alongside Plato's, we shall have to conclude that while there is indeed a progress in clarity and precision of knowledge of the order of being, the leap over the bounds of the finite into the perfection of actual knowledge is impossible. If a thinker attempts it, he is not advancing philosophy, but abandoning it to become a gnostic. Hegel conceals the leap by translating *philosophia* and *gnosis* into German so that he can shift from one to the other by playing on the word "knowledge." This wordplay is structurally analogous to Plato's in the *Phaedrus.* But the philosophic wordplay serves to illuminate the thought, while the gnostic wordplay is designed to conceal the non-thought. This point is worth noting because the German gnostics, especially, like to play with language and hide their non-thought in wordplay.

The result of such transitions—which are in fact leaps—is that the meanings of words are changed. The gnostic program that Hegel successfully carries out retains for itself the name "philosophy," and the speculative system in which the gnostic unfolds his will to make himself master of being insists on calling itself "science."

27. Plato, *Phaedrus,* 278d.

Philosophy springs from the love of being; it is man's loving endeavor to perceive the order of being and attune himself to it. Gnosis desires dominion over being; in order to seize control of being the gnostic constructs his system. The building of systems is a gnostic form of reasoning, not a philosophical one.

But the thinker can seize control of being with his system only if being really lies within his grasp. As long as the origin of being lies beyond the being of this world; as long as eternal being cannot be completely penetrated with the instrument of world-immanent, finite cognition; as long as divine being can be conceived of only in the form of the *analogia entis,* the construction of a system will be impossible. If this venture is to be seriously launched at all, the thinker must first eliminate these inconveniences: he must so interpret being that on principle it lies within the grasp of his construct. Here is Hegel addressing himself to this problem:

> According to my view, which will have to be justified only through the presentation of the system itself, everything depends on comprehending and expressing the true as *subject* no less than as *substance*.[28]

The conditions required for the solution are formulated just as for a mathematical problem: if being is at one and the same time substance and subject, then, of course, truth lies within the grasp of the apprehending subject. But, we must ask, are substance and subject really identical? Hegel dispenses with this question by declaring that the truth of his "view" is proven if he can justify it "through the presentation of the system." If, therefore, I can build a system, the truth of its premise is thereby established; that I can build a system on a false premise is not even considered. The system is justified by the fact of its construction; the possibility of calling into question the construction of systems, as such, is not acknowledged. That the form of science is the system must be assumed as beyond all

28. Hegel, Phänomenologie, p. 19 [Baillie, p. 80].

question. We are confronted here with the same phenomenon of the suppression of questions that we met in Marx. But we now see more clearly that an essential connection exists between the suppression of questions and the construction of a system. Whoever reduces being to a system cannot permit questions that invalidate systems as a form of reasoning.[29]

5

The essential connection between the *libido dominandi,* the system, and the prohibition of questions, although by no means completely worked out, has been made clear by the testimony of the gnostics themselves. Let us return now for the last time to Marx's prohibition against questions.

We recall that Marx un-Socratically breaks off the dialogue with his philosophical interrogator with a ukase. But though he refuses to go any further into the arguments, he is still very careful to base his refusal on the logic of his system. He does not simply dismiss the questioner; he directs him to the path of reason. When the man brings up the problem of the *arche,* Marx admonishes: "Ask yourself whether that progression exists as such for rational thought."[30] Let this person become reasonable; then he will stop his questioning. For Marx, however, reason is not the reason of man but, in the perversion of symbols, the standpoint of his system. His questioner is supposed to cease to be man: he is to become socialist man. Marx thus posits that his construct of the process of being (which comprises the historical process) represents reality. He takes the historical evolution of man into socialist man—which is part of his conceptual construct—and inserts it into his encounters with others; he

29. An analysis of Hegel's "philosophy of history" will reveal the same gnostic program that we have seen in the *Phänomenologie.* See the Note on Hegel's "Philosophy of World History," *infra,* pp. 77–80.

30. Marx, *"Nationalökonomie und Philosophie,"* p. 306 [Bottomore, p. 166].

calls upon the man who questions the assumptions of his system to enter into the system and undergo the evolution it prescribes. In the clash between system and reality, reality must give way. The intellectual swindle is justified by referring to the demands of the historical future, which the gnostic thinker has speculatively projected in his system.

The position of the gnostic thinker derives its authority from the power of being. He is the herald of being, which he interprets as approaching us from the future. This interpretation of being is no doubt active in the speculation of Marx and Nietzsche, but it is not yet worked out in all its consequences. It remained for that ingenious gnostic of our own time, Martin Heidegger, to think the problem through, under the heading of "fundamental ontology." The following examples of speculation on being are taken from his *Einführung in die Metaphysik.*

In Heidegger's speculation being is interpreted on the basis of the original Greek meaning of *parousia* as presence (*An-wesen*).[31] Being is not to be understood statically, as substance, but actively, as presence, in the sense of a coming into presence, as an emerging or appearing—somewhat in the way a ruler makes an appearance or is present. The essence of being as *actio* is a dominating power wherein being creates for itself a world; and it creates this world through man.[32] Man is to be understood historically as an existence that can either open or shut itself to the domination of being. In the historical process, therefore, there can be times of falling away from essential being into the nonessential, whence human existence can find its way back only by opening itself again to the parousia of being. Applying these possibilities to contemporary history, Heidegger decides—as did Marx and Nietzsche in their cruder fashion—that today we in the Western world live in a period of nonessential existence. Hence, the

---

31. Martin Heidegger, *Einführung in die Metaphysik,* 2nd ed. (Tübingen, 1958), p. 46 [*An Introduction to Metaphysics,* trans. Ralph Manheim (New Haven, 1950); Anchor Books edition (Garden City, New York, 1961), p. 50].

32. *Ibid.,* p. 47 [Manheim, p. 51].

future of the West depends on our opening ourselves again to the essential power of being. Heavy with fate fall the formulas: "This means leading man's historical existence (*Dasein*) . . . in the totality of the history alloted us, back to the power of being which originally was to have been opened up"; or: That which is referred to by the word "being" holds "the spiritual fate of the West."[33]

Heidegger's speculation occupies a significant place in the history of Western gnosticism. The construct of the closed process of being; the shutting off of immanent from world-transcendent being; the refusal to acknowledge the experiences of *philia, eros, pistis* (faith), and *elpis* (hope)—which were described and named by the Hellenic philosophers—as the ontic events wherein the soul participates in transcendent being and allows itself to be ordered by it; the refusal, thus, to acknowledge them as the events in which philosophy, especially Platonic philosophy, has its origin; and finally, the refusal to permit the very idea of a construct of a closed process of being to be called into question in the light of these events—all of this was, in varying degrees of clarity, doubtless to be found in the speculative gnostics of the nineteenth century. But Heidegger has reduced this complex to its essential structure and purged it of period-bound visions of the future. Gone are the ludicrous images of positivist, socialist, and super man. In their place Heidegger puts being itself, emptied of all content, to whose approaching power we must submit. As a result of this refining process, the nature of gnostic speculation can now be understood as the symbolic expression of an anticipation of salvation in which the power of being replaces the power of God and the parousia of being, the Parousia of Christ.

6

This completes the analysis. There remains only the task of defining the results conceptually and terminologically.

33. *Ibid.*, p. 32 [Manheim, pp. 34–35].

For this purpose we shall take over from Heidegger's interpretation of being the term "parousia," and speak of parousiasm as the mentality that expects deliverance from the evils of the time through the advent, the coming in all its fullness, of being construed as immanent. We can then speak of the men who express their parousiasm in speculative systems as parousiastic thinkers, of their structures of thought as parousiastic speculations, of the movements connected with some of these thinkers as parousiastic mass movements, and of the age in which these movements are socially and politically dominant as the age of parousiasm. We thus acquire a concept and a terminology for designating a phase of Western gnosticism that have hitherto been lacking. Moreover, by conceiving of it as parousiastic we can distinguish this phase more adequately than heretofore from the preceding chiliastic phase of the Middle Ages and the Renaissance, when the gnostic movements expressed themselves in terms of the Judaeo-Christian apocalypse.[34] The long history of postclassical Western gnosticism thus appears in its continuity as the history of Western sectarianism.

In the Middle Ages this movement could still be kept below the threshold of revolution. Today it has become, not, to be sure, the power of being, but world power. To break the spell of this world and its power—each of us in himself—is the great task at which we all must work. Political science can assist in exorcising the demons—in the modest measure of effectiveness that our society grants to *episteme* and its therapy.

---

34. For the history of the chiliastic phase, see Norman Cohn, *The Pursuit of the Millennium*, 2nd ed. (New York, 1961).

III

THE MURDER OF GOD

OUR ANALYSIS OF parousiastic *doxa* began with the Marxian texts that have to do with the prohibition of questions. The examination was based on these passages because in them the motives, symbols, and patterns of thought of the gnostic mass movements of our time can be seen in rare concentration. It would be difficult to find another document of modern gnosticism that in power and clarity of expression, in intellectual vigor and ingenious determination, would compare with the manuscript of the young Marx. Nevertheless, the selection has a disadvantage in that one of the most powerful motives of the speculation does not stand out with a distinctness in keeping with its actual importance. This is the motive of the murder of God.

The aim of parousiastic gnosticism is to destroy the order of being, which is experienced as defective and unjust, and through man's creative power to replace it with a perfect and just order. Now, however the order of being may be understood—as a world dominated by cosmic-divine powers in the civilizations of the Near and Far East, or as the creation of a world-transcendent God in Judaeo-Christian symbolism, or as an essential order of being in philosophical contemplation—it remains something that is given, that is not under man's control. In order, therefore, that the attempt to create a new world may seem to make sense, the givenness of the order of being must be obliterated; the order of being must be interpreted, rather, as essentially under man's control. And taking control of being further requires that the transcendent origin of being be obliterated: it requires the decapitation of being—the murder of God.

The murder of God is committed speculatively by explaining divine being as the work of man. Let us consider what Nietzsche's Zarathustra has to say on this point: "Alas, my brothers, that God whom I created was human work and human madness, like all gods."[35] Man should stop creating gods because this sets absurd limits to his will and action; and he should realize that the gods he has already created have in fact been created by him. "Let will to truth mean this to you: that everything be changed into the humanly conceivable, the humanly visible, the humanly sensible." This demand also extends to the world, which of old was understood to have been created by God: "What you called 'the world' shall be created only by you: it shall be your reason, your image, your will, your love."[36] "God is a conjecture"—but man's conjectures should not go beyond his creative will,[37] and they should be limited "to the conceivable." There may be no being or image of being that might make human will and thought appear finite: "Neither into the incomprehensible could you have been born, nor into the irrational." In order to appear the unlimited master of being, man must so delimit being that limitations are no longer evident. And why must this magic act be performed? The answer is: "*If* there were gods, how could I endure not being a god! *Therefore,* there are no gods."[38]

It does not suffice, therefore, to replace the old world of God with a new world of man: the world of God itself must have been a world of man, and God a work of man which can therefore be destroyed if it prevents man from reigning over the order of being. The murder of God must be made retroactive speculatively. This is the reason man's "being-of-himself" *(Durchsichselbstsein)* is the

35. Nietzsche, *Also sprach Zarathustra, in Werke,* VI, 42 [Cowan, p. 27].
36. *Ibid.,* p. 124 [Cowan, p. 84].
37. *Ibid.,* p. 123 [Cowan, p. 84].
38. *Ibid.,* p. 124 [Cowan, p. 85].

principal point in Marx's gnosis. And he gets his speculative support from the explanation of nature and history as a process in
which man creates himself to his full stature. The murder of God,
then, is of the very essence of the gnostic re-creation of the order
of being. Like the Promethean hatred of the gods, the murder of God
is a general possibility in human response to God. It is not
confined to parousiastic speculation. In order to clarify the
phenomenon we shall first describe it in the relatively simple
form in which it appears in the golem legends of the Cabbala
of the twelfth and early thirteenth centuries. The legends have
been made available by Gerschom Scholem in his article *"Die
Vorstellung vom Golem in ihren tellurischen und magischen
Beziehungen."*[39]
The late twelfth-century commentary of Pseudo-Saadia on the
book Yezirah includes the golem legend in the following form:

> Thus is it said in the Midrash, that Jeremiah and Ben Sira
> made a man by means of the book Yezirah; and on his brow
> was the word *emeth,* the name that He had uttered over the
> creature that was the perfection of all his work. But that man
> erased the *aleph* so as to say that God alone is truth and he had
> to die.[40]

The Hebrew word *emeth* means "truth." If the first of its three
consonants is crossed out (in Hebrew the initial sound of the word
emeth is represented by a consonant), *meth* is left. *Meth* means
"dead." The adepts made the man "by means of the book
Yezirah"—that is, by means of a magic operation with the letters of

---

39. *Eranos Jahrbuch 1953*, XXII (Zurich, 1954), 235–89 ["The Idea of the Golem,"
On the Kabbalah and Its Symbolism, trans. Ralph Manheim (New York, 1965),
pp. 158–204].
40. *Ibid.*, pp. 259–60 [*On the Kabbalah*, pp. 178–79].

the Hebrew alphabet. This is essentially the same kind of operation as Marx's creation of "socialist man" by means of gnostic speculation. The golem legend now sheds additional light on its nature. In view of the reality of the order of being in which we live, Marx's prohibition of questions had to be characterized as an attempt to protect the "intellectual swindle" of his speculation from exposure by reason; but from the standpoint of the adept Marx the swindle was the "truth" that he had created through his speculation, and the prohibition of questions was designed to defend the truth of the system against the unreason of men. The curious tension between first and second reality, first and second truth, on the pneumopathological nature of which we have remarked, is now revealed to be the tension between the order of God and magic. But this tension, which results from magic's will to power, can be eliminated. For what does the golem do, bearing, like Adam, the man whom God created, the seal of truth on its forehead? It erases the letter *aleph* in order to warn the adepts that the truth is God's; the second truth is death: the golem dies.

The implications of the tension, as well as the means of its resolution, are set forth in greater detail in another version of the golem legend, which is to be found in an early thirteenth-century Cabbalistic text attributed to Juda ben Bathyra. The first part of the legend reads as follows:

> The prophet Jeremiah was alone, working with the book Yezirah. There came a voice from heaven saying, "Obtain for yourself a companion." He went to his son Sira, and they studied the book for three years. Then they set to work on the alphabets, according to the Cabbalistic principles of combination, compilation, and word formation; and there was created unto them a man on whose brow were the words: *YHWH Elohim Emeth*. But there was a knife in the hand of that newly created man with which he scratched out the *aleph* from *emeth;* this left *meth*. Thereupon, Jeremiah

rent his garments and said: "Why do you scratch out the *aleph* from *emeth?*"[41]

Important aspects of magic creation that were only implied in the first legend are now clarified. The second golem carries on its forehead the seal "God is truth." With the effacing of the letter *aleph* it becomes the proclamation "God is dead." After this deed, however, the second golem does not die as did its predecessor. It remains standing there, the knife it used for the murder in its hand. It goes on living and bears the new seal on its brow.

Jeremiah rends his clothing—in the ritual gesture of horror before an act of blasphemy. He asks his creature the meaning of its action, and receives this answer:

I will tell you a parable. There was an architect who built many houses, towns, and squares. But no one could imitate his art and match his knowledge and skill, until two persons prevailed upon him. He then taught them the secret of his art, and they now knew all the proper techniques. When they had acquired his secret and his abilities, they began to badger him until they broke with him and became architects like him; only, things for which he took a thaler they made for six groschen. When people noticed this, they ceased to honor the artist, but honored them instead and gave them the commission when they needed a building. Similarly, God has created you in his image, likeness, and form. But now that you have created a man as He did, it will be said, There is no God in the world other than these two![42]

Gerschom Scholem interprets the legend to mean that a successful creation of a golem would be the prelude to the "death of God";

41. *Ibid.*, p. 261 [*On the Kabbalah*, p. 180].
42. *Ibid.*, pp. 261–62 [*On the Kabbalah*, p. 180].

the hubris of the creator would turn against God. The adept Jeremiah is of the same opinion, and he therefore asks the golem for the way out of this dreadful situation. He then receives from it the formula for the destruction of the magic creature, uses it, "and before their eyes that man became dust and ashes." Jeremiah asks the relevant question; and when he gets an answer that should induce him to destroy his work, he does not suppress the question, but goes ahead and destroys his work.

The legend concludes with Jeremiah saying:

Truly, these things should only be studied in order to recognize the might and omnipotence of the creator of this world and not with the intention of bringing them to pass.[43]

The murder of God in parousiastic gnosticism is a well known and thoroughly explored phenomenon. But many things generally understood under the headings "dialectics of consciousness," "point of view of immanence," "will to pure immanence," and the like sound different with the golem legend in mind. Again, within the scope of this essay, only an illustrative analysis can be attempted. Nietzsche's famous aphorism 125 from *Die fröhliche Wissenschaft* can serve as doxic material. It bears the title "The Madman."[44] Nietzsche carefully constructed the aphorism to set forth the spiritual action that constitutes the murder of God. We shall go through the various phases of this movement of the spirit.

In the bright morning the madman runs out into the marketplace with a lantern crying, "I seek God! I seek God!" Nietzsche thus begins by changing Diogenes' symbolism: the philosopher in search of man has become the madman in search of God. The meaning of the

---

43. *Ibid.*, p. 262 [*On the Kabbalah*, p. 180].

44. Nietzsche, No. 125, *Die fröhliche Wissenschaft*, in *Werke*, V (Leipzig, 1900), 163–64 [*The Gay Science*, in *The Portable Nietzsche*, ed. Kauffmann, pp. 95–96].

change is not immediately clear. The philosophical seeker might well find men in the marketplace; but is that the place to look for God? If we assume that Nietzsche has made an intelligible construct, then we are forced to ask whether the madman is really seeking God; and we thus anticipate the underlying significance of the change in the symbol, which becomes apparent as the aphorism progresses.

The seeker finds in the marketplace just what one would expect to find in a marketplace—men. But these men are of a special breed: "They do not believe in God." They greet his search with laughter and ridicule: "Did he get lost?" they ask; "or is he in hiding? Is he afraid of us? Has he taken a ship? emigrated?"

The madman exclaims to the unbelievers:

Whither has he gone? I will tell you. *We have killed him*—you and I! We are all his murderers.

And how was such a deed possible?

How were we able to drink up the sea? . . . What did we do when we unchained this earth from its sun? Whither is it moving now? Whither are we moving? Away from all suns? . . . Are we not wandering as through an infinite nothingness?

But the deed is done. The murder of God cannot be undone:

God is dead! God will stay dead!

With this outcry the aphorism moves beyond the golem legend. The murder of God is seen for what it is, but the murderer stands by his action. The new creature who committed the murder does not recognize his own death in what happened. The golem lives. "The holiest and mightiest thing the world has yet possessed has bled to death under our knives." The golem stands there, the knife in his hand, ready for other feats.

And what is he seeking with his knife? The God who has already bled to death? No, he seeks "consolation":

> How are we to find consolation, we, the murderers of all murderers? . . . With what water could we cleanse ourselves? . . . Is not the greatness of this deed too great for us?

Nietzsche's questioning recalls the situation in the golem legend, but the golem's instructions to undo the magic murder of God have already been rejected. The madman does not go backward, but forward: if the deed is too great for man, then man must rise up above himself to the greatness of the deed:

> Must we not ourselves become gods just to seem worthy of it? There has never been a greater deed; and whoever is born after us will, because of this act, belong to a higher history than all previous history!

Who murders God will himself become God—the warning of the parable in the second golem legend.

The parable is a warning (and is so understood by the adepts in the legend) because man cannot become God. If he tries, in the process of self-idolization he will become a demon willfully shutting himself off from God. But Nietzsche wishes to continue on just this path. When the madman finishes his speech, his listeners, the unbelievers, are silent and look at him strangely. Then he throws his lantern on the ground and says:

> I have come too soon; my time has not yet come. This stupendous event is still wandering on its way. . . . Deeds need time—even after they have been done—to be seen and heard.

This deed is still farther from them than the remotest stars—
and yet they have done it themselves!

The underlying significance of the Diogenes symbolism is now clear. The new Diogenes does seek God, but not the God who is dead: he seeks the new god in the men who have murdered the old one—he seeks the superman. The madman is therefore looking for man, but not the man of the philosopher: he is looking for the being that springs from the magic of the murder of God. It is necessary to elucidate this symbolism, for, in the conscientious efforts in behalf of Nietzsche's "philosophical" intentions, it is all too often forgotten that the interpreter of a magic *opus* need not, to put it bluntly, be taken in by the magic. It is not enough to examine the symbol of the superman on the basis of the texts and determine the meaning Nietzsche intended; for the symbol occurs in a context of magic. What really takes place in the order of being when this magic is practiced must also be determined. The nature of a thing cannot be changed; whoever tries to "alter" its nature destroys the thing. Man cannot transform himself into a superman; the attempt to create a superman is an attempt to murder man. Historically, the murder of God is not followed by the superman, but by the murder of man: the deicide of the gnostic theoreticians is followed by the homicide of the revolutionary practitioners.

The transition to revolutionary practice is evidenced in the propositions with which Marx opens his *Kritik der Hegelschen Rechtsphilosophie* (1843). The argument is set down so clearly that it scarcely requires commentary.

As in Nietzsche, the magic *opus* presupposes the murder of God: "The critique of religion is the pre-supposition of all critique." God was never anything but a human product. The critique of religion yields this revelation and thereby restores man to the fullness of his nature:

The foundation of irreligious critique is this: *Man makes religion*; religion does not make man. Indeed, religion is man's self-consciousness and self-awareness insofar as he has either not yet found himself or has lost himself again.[45]

Once this relationship has been grasped, the reality of man will manifest itself again:

Man, who sought a superman in the imaginary reality of heaven and found only a *reflection* of himself, will no longer be inclined to find just a *semblance* of himself, just a non-man, where he seeks and must seek his true reality.[46]

Marx is a great deal closer to Nietzsche in these remarks than the use of the symbol "superman" for God might at first reading lead one to suppose. For God, of course, does not exist. "God" is, as in Feuerbach's psychology of religion, the projection of the best in man into a supernatural world. But though the projection in the supernatural is illusionary, this does not mean that the content of the projection is also an illusion. The best in man is real; it must—and here Marx goes beyond the psychology of projection, which exposes religion as an illusion—be drawn back into man. The Marxian *homo novus* is not a man without religious illusions, but one who has taken God back into his being. The "non-man," who has illusions, becomes fully human by absorbing the "superman." In reality, therefore, the new man is, like Nietzsche's superman, the man who has made himself God.

When through the critique of religion man has taken God back

45. Marx, *"Zur Kritik der Hegelschen Rechtsphilosophie. Einleitung,"* in Karl Marx, *Der Historische Materialismus: Die Frühschriften,* p. 263 ["Contribution to the Critique of Hegel's Philosophy of Right. Introduction," in Bottomore, p. 43].
46. *Ibid.*

into himself and has thereby come into full possession of his powers, the critique of politics begins:

> The summons to abandon illusions about his condition is a *summons to abandon a condition that requires illusions.* The critique of religion is therefore *in embryo the critique of the vale of tears* of which religion is the *halo.*[47]
>
> The struggle against religion is therefore indirectly a struggle against *that world* of which religion is the spiritual *aroma.*[48]

Real man "is the *world of man*—the state, society."[49] Only when this world is perverted does it produce the perverted world consciousness of religion:

> Religion is the groan of the oppressed creature, the heart of a heartless world, the spirit of a spiritless condition. It is the *opium* of the people.[50]

It is therefore the task of history,

> . . . once the *world beyond truth* has disappeared, to establish the *truth of this world.*[51]
>
> Thus, the critique of heaven is transformed into the critique of earth; the *critique of religion,* into the *critique of law;* the *critique of theology,* into the *critique of politics.*[52]

The transformed critique is no longer theory, but practice:

47. *Ibid.,* p. 264 [Bottomore, p. 44].
48. *Ibid.,* [Bottomore, p. 43].
49. *Ibid.,* p. 263 [Bottomore, p. 43].
50. *Ibid.,* p. 264 [Bottomore, p. 43–44].
51. *Ibid.* [Bottomore, p. 44].
52. *Ibid.,* p. 265 [Bottomore, p. 44].

Its subject is its *enemy*, which it seeks not to refute, but to *annihilate*. . . . It no longer acts as an *end in itself*, but only as a *means*. Its essential emotion is *indignation*; its essential task is *denunciation*.[53]

Here speaks the will to murder of the gnostic magician. The bonds of reality have been broken. One's fellowman is no longer a partner in being; critique is no longer rational debate. Sentence has been passed; the execution follows.

Marx's critical proclamations refer back to Hegel. Let us turn again to the *Phänomenologie*, that *magnum opus* of the murder of God. We can only offer some reflections on it. A thorough consideration and analysis is impossible in the present context, for it is a rigorously constructed system of more than five hundred pages. The first sentence states the subject of speculation and its limits:

The knowledge that is first or immediately our object can be nothing else but that which is itself immediate knowledge— *knowledge* of the *immediate* or *existent*.[54]

The restriction of the order of being is made even more explicit:

I, *this particular person*, am *certain* of *this* thing, not because *I* have developed as consciousness herewith and in various ways prompted thought; nor because *the thing* of which I am certain was, because of a number of distinct qualities, a complex of relations within itself or a manifold of relations with other things. Neither has anything to do with the truth of sensible certitude.[55]

The nature of the order of being as it is given, together with man's

53. *Ibid.*, p. 266 [Bottomore, p. 46].
54. Hegel, *Phänomenologie des Geistes*, p. 79 [Baillie, p. 149].
55. *Ibid.*, pp. 79–80 [Baillie, pp. 149–50].

place in it, is obliterated: the being of world and ego is restricted to the knowledge of the immediate or existent; questions about the context of the order of being in which this knowledge occurs are declared irrelevant; the prohibition of questions is solemnly made a principle of the speculation. From this beginning the substance of the order of being—which, for the philosopher, is something given—is systematically construed as a succession of phases of consciousness which proceed in dialectical development from the initial consciousness of sensible certitude. In its language the *Phänomenologie* is philosophical; in its substance and intention it is radically anti-philosophical. It must be recognized as a work of magic—indeed, it is one of the great magic performances.

Nothing can be plucked out of this masterpiece of rigorous magical speculation without destroying the meaning of the whole. Therefore, we can only advert to a few passages where the theme of the murder of God—the object of the whole enterprise—appears. The most prominent text takes up the death of Christ:

> The death of the Mediator is not just the death of his *natural* aspect . . . ; what dies is not merely the dead husk that has been stripped from the essence, but the *abstraction* of divine being as well. . . . The death of this mental image (*Vorstellung*), therefore, comprises at the same time the death of the *abstraction of divine being*, which is not established as self. This death is the unhappy consciousness' painful feeling that *God himself has died.*[56]

What seems here to be a simple statement—the mere observation of a fact—is actually something more. For God has died because he was no more than a phase of consciousness that is now outmoded. And it is outmoded because consciousness in its dialectical progress has gone beyond it. The death of God is not an event, but

56. *Ibid.*, p. 546 [Baillie, pp. 781–82].

the feat of a dialectician. The "harsh utterance" that God has died marks

> . . . the return of consciousness to the depth of the night
> where the ego = ego, where the night no longer distin-
> guishes or knows anything outside of itself. . . . This knowl-
> edge is thus the *spiritualization* whereby substance, its
> abstraction and lifelessness having died, has become subject,
> whereby it has therefore *actually* become simple and universal
> self-consciousness.[57]

What at the stage of "religion" was still a mental image of an other has here become the inherent "action of the self." This last form of the spirit is absolute knowledge.[58] To be sure, religion expresses what spirit is earlier in time than does science; "but science alone is the spirit's true knowledge of itself."[59] When the spirit appears to consciousness in the medium of the concept, or rather is generated by consciousness in this medium, it has become "science."[60] The spirit as knowing what it is does not exist until it has completed the task.

> . . . of providing for its consciousness the form of its essence
> and in this manner of putting its *self-consciousness* on a level
> with its consciousness.[61]

Or, to put it all more simply and directly, the spirit as system requires the murder of God; and, conversely, in order to commit the murder of God the system is fashioned.

The *Phänomenologie* ends with a meditation on history as the spirit attaining its self-consciousness in time:

57. *Ibid.* [Baillie, p. 782].
58. *Ibid.*, p. 556 [Baillie, p. 797].
59. *Ibid.*, p. 559 [Baillie, p. 801].
60. *Ibid.*, p. 556 [Baillie, p. 798].
61. *Ibid.*, p. 557 [Baillie, p. 799].

This process of becoming presents a slow movement and succession of spirits, a gallery of images, each endowed with the
entire wealth of the spirit and moving so slowly just because
the self must penetrate and digest all this wealth of its
substance.[62]

A realm of spirits unfolds in the temporal existence of history,
in which each spirit takes over the realm of the world from the
preceding one, until, in the final phase of self-consciousness, the
completely unfolded history has become "internalizing recollection" (*Er-Innerung*). The goal—absolute knowledge—is attained
through

   . . . the recollection of the spirits as they are in themselves and
   as they accomplish the organization of their realm.[63]

The preservation of this succession of spirits according to the tem-
porality of their existence is history; their preservation as a
comprehended organization is the science of emergent knowledge.
Both together, as history comprehended,

   . . . form the recollection and the golgotha of the absolute
   spirit, the actuality, truth, and certainty of its throne, without
   which it would be a lifeless, solitary thing; only—
      from the chalice of this realm of spirits
      its infinity foams out to it.[64]

When we were analyzing Nietzsche's aphorism we had occasion
to remark that the interpreter of a magic *opus* need not himself be
taken in by the magic. Let us therefore step out of the magic circle

62. *Ibid.,* p. 563 [Baillie, p. 807].
63. *Ibid.,* p. 564 [Baillie, p. 808].
64. *"aus dem Kelche dieses Geisterreiches*
   schäumt ihm seine Unendlichkeit." Ibid.

of the *opus* back onto the solid ground of reality. Let us consider what is taking place in the order of being as Hegel concludes his work at the golgotha of the spirit. If we attempt to summarize his summary for this purpose, we shall have to say: On the grave of the murdered God the golem is celebrating a ghastly ritual—a kind of triumphal dance accompanied with chant. The goal has been attained. The "revelation of the depth" has been successfully carried out. But the depth is nothing but the "absolute concept," and "this revelation" is therefore the "cancellation" (*Aufheben*) of the depth. And there is no other revelation. Then sounds the chant:

> from the chalice of this realm of spirits
> its infinity foams out to it.

These last two lines of the work, which are printed as if they were poetry, alter the conclusion of Schiller's poem "Friendship":

> Though the Supreme Being found no equal,
> From the chalice of the whole realm of souls
> There foams *to him*—infinity.[65]

This is the closing act of the gnostic destruction of reality. For the fate of the order of being when gnostic magicians lay hands on it Hegel has found a fitting symbol: the mutilation of a poem.[66]

---

65. "*Fand das höchste Wesen shon kein Gleiches,*
    aus dem Kelch des ganzen Seelenveiches
    Schäumt ihm—*die Unendlichkeit.*"

66. For a more extensive analysis of this mutilation, see Alexandre Kojève, *Introduction à la lecture de Hegel* (Paris, 1947), p. 442.

IV

NOTE ON HEGEL'S "PHILOSOPHY OF WORLD HISTORY"

I N THE FOREGOING analysis I have illustrated Hegel's program of advancing from philosophy to gnosis, as well as the conditions required for building his system, with passages from the *Phänomenologie* only—that is, on the level of "philosophy itself." Hegel reiterates essentially the same formulas on the level of the "philosophy of world history." I shall now give the parallel passages from the "Second Draft" of the *Philosophische Weltgeschichte* of 1830 (in *Die Vernunft in der Geschichte*, ed. Johannes Hoffmeister [Hamburg, 1955]).

1) Hegel distinguishes between "philosophy itself" and the "philosophy of world history." The philosopher approaches the interpretation of world history with the "presupposition" that "reason governs the world and that, therefore, in world history things have come to pass rationally."

In philosophy itself this is not a presupposition; there, it is *demonstrated* by speculative cognition that reason—we can accept this term without going into the question of the relationship to God—which is substance as well as infinite *power*, is itself the *infinite matter* of all natural and spiritual life and is *infinite form* as well, the actualization of this matter which is its content. (p. 28.)

The relationship of reason to God, which in this sentence remains undefined, becomes apparent as the "Second Draft" progresses. Under the denomination "idea," reason is the absolute revealing itself:

> Now, that this same idea is the true, the eternal, the absolutely powerful, that it reveals itself in the world, and that nothing is manifested in the world but it, its majesty and glory—this, as has been said, is proved in philosophy and is *presupposed* here as proved. (p. 29.)

That the attributes are intended as divine and that God is identified with reason which unfolds itself in speculation and history is made clear in the following passage:

> The *world spirit* is the spirit of the world as it explains itself in human consciousness; men are related to this spirit as individual parts to the whole that is their substance. And this world spirit conforms to the divine spirit, which is absolute spirit. Insofar as God is omnipresent, he is in every man, he appears in everyone's consciousness; and this is the world spirit. (p. 60.)

2) Since the idea is identical with the self-revealing deity, the design of progressing from philosophy to gnosis is carried over from the sphere of "philosophy itself" to the "philosophy of world history." It is the philosopher's task to advance from the partial revelation of God through Christ to the complete comprehension of God. He is committed to this task by "Holy Scripture," according to which "it is the spirit that leads to truth, that it may know all

things, even the depths of the godhead" (pp. 40–41). The task itself is formulated in the following passage:

> In the Christian religion God has revealed himself—that is, he has made known to men what he is, so that he is no longer something concealed and secret. With the possibility of knowing God it becomes incumbent upon us to do so; and the development of thinking spirit, which has proceeded from this foundation, from the revelation of the divine being, must ultimately mature to the point where what was in the first instance presented to feeling and imagining spirit is grasped in thought. Whether the time has come for such knowledge necessarily depends on whether the ultimate goal of the world has finally made its appearance in actuality in a universally valid and conscious way. (p. 45.)

3) The program of exhaustively penetrating the depths of the godhead through its unfolding in world history is tied to the condition that the ultimate goal of the world has indeed fully unfolded in world history and become comprehensible. Just as on the level of "philosophy itself" the truth of Hegel's "view" is justified by "the presentation of the system," so on the level of the "philosophy of world history" the validity of his thesis about complete revelation is proved by the execution of the program:

> Thus, the result of the study of world history itself has been and is that things have come to pass rationally, that world history has been the rational, necessary course of the world spirit. (p. 30.) [Note the perfect tense.]

That a last end is the governing principle in the events of peoples, that reason is in world history—not the reason of a particular subject, but the divine, absolute reason—is a truth that we presuppose; its proof is the treatise on world history itself: the image and the work of reason. (p. 29.)

PART TWO

Ersatz Religion

The Gnostic Mass Movements of Our Time

ERSATZ RELIGION

T HE TERM "GNOSTIC mass movement" is not in common use. Therefore, when one encounters it one expects it first to be defined. This, however, is not possible, since for methodological reasons definitions come at the end of the analytical process and not at the beginning. And if the analysis has been carefully carried out, definitions are no longer of any great importance, for they can provide no more than a summary of the results of the analysis. We shall follow the Aristotelian method and speak first illustratively of the subject to be examined, and then, when it is secured at the common-sense level of our experience, proceed with the analysis.

I

By gnostic movements we mean such movements as progressivism, positivism, Marxism, psychoanalysis, communism, fascism, and national socialism. We are not dealing, therefore, in all of these cases with political mass movements. Some of them would more accurately be characterized as intellectual movements—for example, positivism, neo-positivism, and the variants of psychoanalysis. This draws attention to the fact that mass movements do not represent an autonomous phenomenon and that the difference between masses and intellectual elites is perhaps not so great as is conventionally assumed, if indeed it exists at all. At any rate, in social reality the two types merge. None of the movements cited began as a mass movement; all derived from intellectuals and small groups. Some of them, according to the intentions of their founders, should have grown into political mass movements, but did not. Others, such as neo-positivism or psychoanalysis, were meant to be intellectual movements; but they have had, if not the form, at least the success of political mass movements, in that their theories and jargons have shaped the thinking of millions of people in the Western world, very often without their being aware of it.

A brief outline of Comteian positivism may serve as a representative example of how mass and intellectual movements are connected. Positivism was an intellectual movement that began with Saint-Simon, with Comte and his friends, and was intended by its founders to become a mass movement of worldwide extent. All mankind was expected to compose the fellowship of the positivist congregation under the spiritual leadership of the *"fondateur de la religion de l'humanité."* Comte tried to enter into diplomatic correspondence with Nicholas I, with the Jesuit General, and with the Grand Vizier, in order to in-corporate into positivism Russian Orthodoxy, the Catholic Church, and Islam. Even though these grandiose plans fell through, something significant was achieved. There have been strong positivist movements, especially in South America; and to this day the Republic of Brazil has on its flag the Comteian motto "Order and Progress." Comteian positivism engaged the best minds of the time in Europe. It decidedly influenced John Stuart Mill; and the echo of the Comteian view of history can still be heard in the philosophy of Max Weber, Ernest Cassirer, and Edmund Husserl. Finally, the entire Western world can thank Comte for the word "altruism"—the secular-immanent substitute for "love," which is associated with Christianity: altruism is thebasis of the conception of a brotherhood of man without a father. In the case of

positivism one can see perhaps most clearly how problems concerning intellectual and mass movements converge.

II

We have located the subject of our inquiry at the level of
common sense, and must now proceed to clarify further the
degree to which the movements cited can be characterized as
gnostic.

Again, we cannot give definitions, only allusions to the historical in-
stances. Gnosticism was a religious movement of antiquity. It can be
confirmed as having been approximately contemporary with
Christianity—so contemporary, in fact, that it was assumed for a long
time that gnosis involved no more than a Christian heresy. This notion can no longer be held today. Although there are no gnostic
sources that can be dated with certainty before the birth of Christ,
gnostic influences and terminology are indeed so clearly recognizable
in St. Paul that they must stem from a powerful movement in existence
before his time. On the historical continuity of gnosticism from antiquity to modern times, let it be said here only that the connections in
the development of gnostic sects from those of the eastern
Mediterranean in antiquity through the movements of the high
Middle Ages up to those of the Western Renaissance and Reformation
have been sufficiently clarified to permit us to speak of a continuity.

More important for our purposes than definitions and questions
of genesis are the features by which we can recognize gnostic movements as such. Let us list, therefore, the six characteristics that, taken
together, reveal the nature of the gnostic attitude.

1) It must first be pointed out that the gnostic is dissatisfied with
his situation. This, in itself, is not especially surprising. We all have
cause to be not completely satisfied with one aspect or another of
the situation in which we find ourselves.

2) Not quite so understandable is the second aspect of the gnostic attitude: the belief that the drawbacks of the situation can be attributed to the fact that the world is intrinsically poorly organized. For it is likewise possible to assume that the order of being as it is given to us men (wherever its origin is to be sought) is good and that it is we human beings who are inadequate. But gnostics are not inclined to discover that human beings in general and they themselves in particular are inadequate. If in a given situation something is not as it should be, then the fault is to be found in the wickedness of the world.

3) The third characteristic is the belief that salvation from the evil of the world is possible.

4) From this follows the belief that the order of being will have to be changed in an historical process. From a wretched world a good one must evolve historically. This assumption is not altogether self-evident, because the Christian solution might also be considered—namely, that the world throughout history will remain as it is and that man's salvational fulfillment is brought about through grace in death.

5) With this fifth point we come to the gnostic trait in the narrower sense—the belief that a change in the order of being lies in the realm of human action, that this salvational act is possible through man's own effort.

6) If it is possible, however, so to work a structural change in the given order of being that we can be satisfied with it as a perfect one, then it becomes the task of the gnostic to seek out the prescription for such a change. Knowledge—gnosis—of the method of altering being is the central concern of the gnostic. As the sixth feature of the gnostic attitude, therefore, we recognize the construction of a formula for self and world salvation, as well as the gnostic's readiness to come forward as a prophet who will proclaim his knowledge about the salvation of mankind.

These six characteristics, then, describe the essence of the gnostic attitude. In one variation or another they are to be found in each of the movements cited.

III

For its appropriate expression, the gnostic attitude has produced a rich and multiform symbolism in the modern mass movements. It is so extensive that it cannot be completely described in this essay. We shall deal with only a few of the most important complexes of symbols. Let us begin with that complex of symbols which can be recognized as modifications of the Christian idea of perfection.

This idea represents the insight that human nature does not find its fulfillment in this world, but only in the *visio beatifica,* in supernatural perfection through grace in death. Since, therefore, there is no fulfillment in this world, Christian life on earth takes its special form from the life to come in the next. It is shaped by *sanctificatio,* by the sanctification of life. Two components can be distinguished in the Christian idea of perfection. The first component is that of the movement toward the goal of perfection, which is described by the expression "sanctification of life"—in English Puritanism, by the notion of the *pilgrim's progress.* As movement toward a goal, it is referred to as the *teleological* component. Further, the goal, the *telos,* toward which the movement is directed, is understood as ultimate perfection; and since the goal is a state of highest value, this second component is called the *axiological.* The two components, the teleological and the axiological, were identified by Ernst Troeltsch.

The gnostic mass movements derive their ideas of perfection from the Christian. In accordance with the components just described, there are on principle three possibilities of derivation. In gnostic perfection, which is supposed to come to pass within the historical world, the teleological and axiological components can be immanentized either separately or together. There follow a few examples of the three types of immanentization.

To the first type of derivation, the teleological, belongs progressivism in all variants. When the teleological component is immanentized, the chief emphasis of the gnostic-political idea lies on the forward movement, on the movement toward a goal of perfection in this world. The goal itself need not be understood very precisely; it may consist of no more than the idealization of this or that aspect of the situation, considered valuable by the thinker in question. Eighteenth-century ideas of progress—for example, Kant's or Condorcet's—belong to this teleological variant of gnosis. According to the Kantian idea of progress, humanity is moving in an unending approach toward the goal of a perfect, rational existence in a cosmopolitan society—although, to Kant's credit, it must be said that he was able to find in the unending progress of mankind no salvation for the individual man, and the relevance of progress for the fulfillment of the person therefore seemed doubtful to him. Condorcet was somewhat less patient than Kant. He chose not to leave the perfection of man to the unending progress of history, but to accelerate it through a directorate of intellectuals. However, his progressivist idea thereby approaches the third type, the activist effort toward perfection; for the three types of derivation are rarely found in pure form in the individual gnostic thinkers, but usually in multifarious combinations.

In the second type of derivation, the axiological, the emphasis of the idea falls on the state of perfection in the world. Conditions for a perfect social order are described and worked out in detail and assume the form of an ideal image. Such an image was first sketched by Thomas More in his *Utopia*. But the design for perfection need not always be as carefully worked out as it is in More. Much more common are those depictions of a desirable final state that are designed as negatives of some specific evil in the world. The list of these evils has been familiar since antiquity; it was drawn up by Hesiod. Chiefly, it includes poverty, sickness, death, the necessity for work, and sexual problems. These are the principal categories of the burden of existence, to which correspond the models of society offering specific deliverance from one ill or another. Incomplete notions of perfections of this sort may be called *ideals,* in order to distinguish them from the complete models of the utopian kind.

Under ideals, therefore, should be included fragments of utopias, such as the notion of a society without private property or of one free from the burdens of labor, sickness, or anxiety. It is characteristic of the whole class of these axiological derivatives that they draw up a comparatively lucid picture of the desirable condition, but are concerned only vaguely with the means of bringing it about.

In the third type of derivation the two components are immanentized together, and there is present both a conception of the end goal and knowledge of the methods by which it is to be brought about. We shall speak of cases of this third type as *activist mysticism*. Under activist mysticism belong primarily movements that descend from Auguste Comte and Karl Marx. In both cases one finds a relatively clear formulation of the state of perfection: in Comte, a final state of industrial society under the temporal rule of the managers and the spiritual rule of positivist intellectuals; in Marx, a final state of a classless realm of freedom. And in both cases, there is clarity about the way to perfection: for Comte, through the transformation of man into his highest form, positivist man; for Marx, through the revolution of the proletariat and the transformation of man into the communist superman.

IV

A second complex of symbols that runs through modern gnostic mass movements was created in the speculation on history of Joachim of Flora at the end of the twelfth century.

Joachim's historical speculation was directed against the then reigning philosophy of history of St. Augustine. According to the Augustinian construction, the phase of history since Christ was the sixth, the last earthly age—the *saeculum senescens,* the time of the senility of mankind. The present had no earthly future; its meaning was exhausted in a waiting for the end of history through eschatological events. The motives of this view of history are to be sought in the experiences of the fifth century in which it was formed. In the time of Augustine it seemed indeed that, if not *the* world, at least *a* world was approaching its end. But twelfth-century western European man could not be satisfied with the view of a senile world waiting for its end; for his world was quite obviously not in its decline, but, on the contrary, on the upsurge. Population was increasing, areas of settlement were expanding, wealth was growing, cities were being founded, and intellectual life was intensifying, especially through the emergence of the great religious orders since Cluny. The idea of senility must have seemed preposterous to this vital, expanding age, relishing the exercise of its civilizing powers.

Like Joachim himself, his speculation arose out of the thriving religious orders. He projected his view of history on a trinitarian scheme. World history was a consequence of three great ages—those of the Father, the Son, and the Holy Spirit. The first age lasted from the Creation to the birth of Christ; the second, that of the Son, began with Christ. But the age of the Son was not, as Augustine had it, mankind's last; rather, it was to be followed by an additional one, that of the Holy Spirit. We can recognize, even in this thoroughly Christian context, the first symptoms of the idea of a post Christian era. Joachim went further and indulged in concrete speculations about the beginning of the age of the Holy Spirit, fixing its inauguration at 1260. And the new age, like the preceding ones, was to be ushered in by the appearance of a leader. As the first age began with Abraham and the second with Christ, so the third was to begin in the year 1260 with the appearance of a *dux e Babylone*.

So ran the Joachitic speculation. It comprises a complex of four symbols which have remained characteristic of the political mass movements of modern times.

The first of these symbols is that of the Third Realm—that is, the conception of a third world-historical phase that is at the same time the last, the age of fulfillment. An extensive class of gnostic ideas comes under the symbol of the three phases. First and foremost would be the humanistic periodization of world history into ancient, medieval, and modern. This classification was derived in its original version from Biondo. It established as the Middle Ages the millennium from the conquest of Rome by the West Goths to the year 1410. Then, in the eighteenth century, the three-phase laws made famous by Turgot and Comte make their appearance: world history is divided into a first theological, a second metaphysical, and a third phase of positive science. In Hegel we encounter a tripartite division of world history according to levels of freedom: antiquity with its oriental despotism, when only one was free; then aristocratic times, when a few were free; and now modern times, when all are free. Marx and Engels applied this tripartite scheme to their question of the proletariat and spoke of a first phase of primitive communism, a second phase of bourgeois class society, and a third of classless society when the final communist realm of freedom is realized. Again, Schelling, in his speculation on history, distinguished three great phases of Christianity: first the Petrine, followed by the Pauline, which will be sealed by the Johannine phase of perfect Christianity.

These are only the principal cases. They are cited to show that the projection of a Third Realm of perfection is in fact a ruling symbol in the self-understanding of modern society and that after several centuries of preparation for final Third Realms, the attempt to bring them into existence by revolutionary action should no longer especially surprise us. The enumeration should further serve to suggest that a type of experience and symbolism that has been built up for centuries will hardly lose its dominant position in Western history overnight.

The second symbol Joachim developed is that of the leader, the *dux,* who appears at the beginning of a new era and through his appearance establishes that era. This symbol was avidly snatched up by Joachim's salvation-seeking contemporaries. The first to fall victim to it was St. Francis of Assisi. He was considered by so many to be the leader to the realm of the Holy Spirit that he felt it necessary to take special measures to guard against this misunderstanding of his entirely orthodox actions. In spite of his pains, belief in St. Francis as the leader of the Third Realm persisted, and had a very strong influence on Dante's conception of such a leader-figure. Moreover, the idea dominated the sectarian movements of the Renaissance and Reformation: their leaders were paracletes possessed by the spirit of God, and their followers were the *homines novi* or *spirituales*. Dante's notion of a *dux* of the new realm emerged again in the period of national socialism and fascism. There exists a German and Italian literature in which Hitler and Mussolini are at times glorified as the leaders foretold by Dante.

In the period of secularization leaders could not be presented as God-possessed paracletes. By the end of the eighteenth century a new symbol, that of the "superman," begins to take the place of the old sectarian categories. The expression—coined by Goethe in *Faust*—is used in the nineteenth century by Marx and Nietzsche to characterize the new man of the Third Realm. The process by which the superman is created is closely related to the movement of the spirit in which the older sectarians drew into themselves the substance of God and transformed themselves into the "godded man," the divinized man. God is understood by the secularist sectarians as a projection of the substance of the human soul into the illusionary spaciousness of the "beyond." Through psychological analysis, this illusion can be dispelled and "God" brought back from his beyond into the human soul from which he sprung. By dispelling the illusion, the divine substance is reincorporated in man, and man becomes superman. The act of taking God back into man, just as among the older sectarians, has the result of creating a human type who experiences himself as existing outside of institutional bonds and obligations. As the main types of the superman we can distinguish the progressivist superman of Condorcet (who even has the hope of an eternal earthly life), the positivist superman of

Comte, the communist superman of Marx, and the Dionysian superman of Nietzsche.

The third of Joachim's symbols is that of the prophet. Joachim assumed that the leader of each age had a precursor, just as Christ had St. John the Baptist. Even the leader out of the Babylonian captivity, who was to appear in 1260, had such a precursor—in this case, Joachim himself. With the creation of the symbol of the precursor, a new type emerges in Western history: the intellectual who knows the formula for salvation from the misfortunes of the world and can predict how world history will take its course in the future. In Joachitic speculation, the intellectual is still deeply immersed in the medium of Christianity, in that Joachim understands himself to be the prophet of the coming, God-sent *dux e Babylone*. In the further course of Western history, the Christian tide recedes, and the prophet, the precursor of the leader, becomes the secularist intellectual who thinks he knows the meaning of history (understood as world-immanent) and can predict the future. In political practice, the figure of the intellectual who projects the image of future history and makes predictions cannot always be clearly separated from that of the leader. In the case of Comte, for example, we doubtless have the figure of a leader before us; but, at the same time, Comte is also the intellectual who prognosticates his own role as leader of world history and, moreover, even transforms himself through the magic of meditative practice from the intellectual into the leader. In the case of communism, also, it is difficult to separate leader and intellectual in the person of a Karl Marx. But in the historical form of the movement, Marx and Engels have been distinguished, by the distance of a generation, as "precursors," from Lenin and Stalin as "leaders," of the realization of the Third Realm.

The fourth of the Joachitic symbols is the community of spiritually autonomous persons. In the spirit of the monasticism of the time, Joachim imagined the Third Realm as a community of monks. In our context, the importance of this image lies in the idea

of a spiritualized mankind existing in community without the me-
diation and support of institutions; for, according to Joachim's
view, the spiritual community of monks was to exist without the
sacramental supports of the Church. In this free community of autonomous persons without institutional organization can be seen
the same symbolism found in modern mass movements, which
imagine the Final Realm as a free community of men after the ex-
tinction of the state and other institutions. The symbolism is most
clearly recognizable in communism, but the idea of democracy also
thrives not inconsiderably on the symbolism of a community of autonomous men.

This concludes our discussion of Joachitic symbolism. In it, we
have one of the great complexes of symbols that became active in
modern political mass movements and has remained so to the present day.

V

The two complexes we have briefly outlined here by no means ex-
haust the symbolic language of the mass movements. In order to
achieve approximate completeness, we would have to add those
that can be traced back to the Latin Averroism and nominalism of
the Middle Ages. But the symbols deriving from the Christian idea
of perfection and Joachitic speculation are doubtless the dominant
ones, to which the others are adjusted. And in both the immanentization of the Christian idea of perfection holds primacy.

This position is ontologically determined by the central importance of the question of immanentization. All gnostic movements
are involved in the project of abolishing the constitution of being,
with its origin in divine, transcendent being, and replacing it with
a world-immanent order of being, the perfection of which lies in
the realm of human action. This is a matter of so altering the structure of the world, which is perceived as inadequate, that a new, sat-

isfying world arises. The variants of immanentization, therefore, are the controlling symbols, to which the other complexes are subordinated as secondary ways of expressing the will to immanentization.

No matter to which of the three variants of immanentization the movements belong, the attempt to create a new world is common to all. This endeavor can be meaningfully undertaken only if the constitution of being can in fact be altered by man. The world, however, remains as it is given to us, and it is not within man's power to change its structure. In order—*not,* to be sure, to make the undertaking possible—but to make it *appear* possible, every gnostic intellectual who drafts a program to change the world must first construct a world picture from which those essential features of the constitution of being that would make the program appear hopeless and foolish have been eliminated. Let us turn, then, to this specific trait of gnostic models of the world. In three representative cases we shall show which factor of reality has been omitted in order to make the possibility of an alteration in the unsatisfactory state of things seem plausible. For our three examples we have chosen Thomas More's *Utopia,* Hobbes's *Leviathan,* and Hegel's construct of history.

In his *Utopia* More traces the image of man and of society that he considers perfect. To this perfection belongs the abolition of private property. Because he had the benefit of an excellent theological education, however, More is well aware that this perfect state cannot be achieved in the world: man's lust for possessions is deeply rooted in original sin, in *superbia* in the Augustinian sense. In the final part of his work when More looks over his finished picture, he has to admit that it would all be possible if only there were not the "serpent of superbia." But there *is* the serpent of superbia—and More would not think of denying it. This raises the question of the peculiar psychopathological condition in which a man like More must have found himself when he drew up a model of the perfect society in history, in full consciousness that it could never be realized because of original sin.

And this opens up the problem of the strange, abnormal spiritual condition of gnostic thinkers, for which we have not as yet developed an adequate terminology in our time. In order, therefore, to be able to speak of this phenomenon, it will be advisable to use the term "pneumopathology," which Schelling coined for this purpose. In a case like More's, we may speak, then, of the pneumopathological condition of a thinker who, in his revolt against the world as it has been created by God, arbitrarily omits an element of reality in order to create the fantasy of a new world.

As More leaves superbia out of his image of man in order to create a utopian order from this new man freed by the intellectual from original sin, so Hobbes leaves out another essential factor in order to be able to construct his *Leviathan*. The factor Hobbes omits is the *summum bonum,* the highest good. Now, Hobbes knows that human action can be considered rational only if it is oriented beyond all intermediate stages of ends and means to a last end, this same *summum bonum.* Hobbes further knows that the *summum bonum* was the primary condition of rational ethics in the classical as well as the scholastic thinkers. Therefore, in the introduction to the *Leviathan* he states explicitly that he proposes to leave the *summum bonum* of the "old thinkers" out of his construct of society. If there is no *summum bonum,* however, there is no point of orientation that can endow human action with rationality. Action, then, can only be represented as motivated by passions, above all, by the passion of aggression, the overcoming of one's fellow man. The "natural" state of society must be understood as the war of all against all, if men do not in free love orient their actions to the highest good. The only way out of the warfare of this passion-conditioned state of nature is to submit to a passion stronger than all others, which will subdue their aggressiveness and drive to dominate and induce them to live in peaceful order. For Hobbes, this passion is the fear of the *summum malum,* the fear of death at the hands of another, to which each man is exposed in his natural state. If men are not moved to live with one another in peace through common love of the divine, highest good, then the fear of the *summum malum* of death must force them to live in an orderly society.

The motives of this strange construct are more clearly discernible in Hobbes than in More. The author of the *Leviathan* formed his image of man and society under the pressure of the Puritan Revolution. He diagnosed the efforts of the Puritan sectarians to set up the Kingdom of God as an expression of the *libido dominandi* of the revolutionary who wants to bend men to his will. The "spirit" that he saw as inspiring these armed prophets of the new world was not the spirit of God, but human lust for power. He then generalized this observation—which was quite accurate in the case of the Puritans—and made the *libido dominandi,* which is the revolt of man against his nature and God, the essential characteristic of human beings. *Every* movement of the spirit became for him a pretext for a movement of the passions. There was absolutely no orientation of human action through love of God, but only motivation through the world-immanent power drive. And these "proud ones," who wanted to rule and pass off their will to power as the will of God, had to be broken by the Leviathan, the "Lord of the Proud," who held them in check with his threat of death and compelled them to accept the peaceful order of society. The result of these assumptions was the same for Hobbes as for More. If men are incapable of ordering their dealings with each other in freedom through love of the *summum bonum,* if society disintegrates into civil war—in fact, into the state of a war of all against all—and if this condition is considered man's "state of nature" from which there is no escape, then the hour has come of the thinker who possesses the formula for the restoration of order and the guarantee of eternal peace. The society that is governed neither by God's will nor its own shall be placed under that of the gnostic thinker. The *libido dominandi* that Hobbes diagnosed in the Puritans celebrates its highest triumph in the construction of a system that denies man the freedom and ability to order his life in society. Through the construction of the system the thinker becomes the only free person—a god, who will deliver man from the evils of the "state of nature." This function of the system is clearer in Hobbes than it was in More because Hobbes recommends his work to a "sovereign" who may read it, ponder it, and act accordingly. More did indeed construct his Utopia; but this humanist's game, dangerous as it was, was still only a game, for More remained aware that the perfect society was, and would always be, "nowhere." But Hobbes takes his construct in dead earnest. He recommends it to a person in power who is to suppress the apparent freedom of the spirit and its order, because in Hobbes's opinion man does not have the real thing.

The third case we shall consider is Hegel's philosophy of history. Let us first state that the term "philosophy of history" may be applied to Hegel's speculation only with reservations. For Hegel's history is not to be found in reality, and the reality of history is not in Hegel. The harmony between construct and history could be achieved in this case, too, only through the omission of an essential factor of reality.

The factor Hegel excludes is the mystery of a history that wends its way into the future without our knowing its end. History as a whole is essentially not an object of cognition; the meaning of the whole is not discernible. Hegel can construct, then, a meaningfully self-contained process of history only by assuming that the revelation of God in history is fully comprehensible. The appearance of Christ was for him the crux of world history; in this decisive epoch God had revealed the Logos—reason—in history. But the revelation was incomplete, and Hegel considered it man's duty to complete the incomplete revelation by raising the Logos to complete clarity in consciousness. This elevation to consciousness is in fact possible through the mind of the philosopher—concretely, through the mind of Hegel: in the medium of the Hegelian dialectic the revelation of God in history reaches its fulfillment. The validity of the construct depends on the assumption that the mystery of revelation and of the course of history can be solved and made fully transparent through the dialectical unfolding of the Logos. We have here a construct closely related to that of Joachim of Flora. Joachim, too, was dissatisfied with the Augustinian waiting for the end; he, too, wanted to have an intelligible meaning in history here and now; and in order to make the meaning intelligible, he had to set himself up as the prophet to whom this meaning was clear. In the same manner, Hegel identifies his human logos with the Logos that is Christ, in order to make the meaningful process of history fully comprehensible.

VI

In the three cases of More, Hobbes, and Hegel, we can establish that the thinker suppresses an essential element of reality in order to be able to construct an image of man, or society, or history to suit his desires. If we now consider the question of why the thinker would thus contradict reality, we shall not find the answer on the level of theoretic argument; for we have obviously gone beyond reason, if the relation to reality is so greatly disturbed that essential elements are on principle excluded from consideration. We must move our inquiry to the psychological level, and a first answer has already yielded itself in the course of our presentation: the will to power of the gnostic who wants to rule the world has triumphed over the humility of subordination to the constitution of being. This answer cannot completely satisfy us, however, for while the will to power has indeed conquered humility, the result of victory is not really the acquisition of power. The constitution of being remains what it is—beyond the reach of the thinker's lust for power. It is not changed by the fact that a thinker drafts a program to change it and fancies that he can implement that program. The result, therefore, is not dominion over being, but a fantasy satisfaction.

Therefore, we must go further and inquire into the psychic gain the thinker receives from the construction of his image and the psychic needs the masses of his followers satisfy through it. From the materials we have presented, it would appear that this gain consists in a stronger certainty about the meaning of human existence, in a new knowledge of the future that lies before us, and in the creation of a more secure basis for action in the future. Assurances of this sort, however, are sought only if man feels uncertain on these points. If we then inquire further about the reasons for the uncertainty, we come upon aspects of the order of being and man's place in it that do indeed give cause for uncertainty—an uncertainty perhaps so hard to bear that it may be acknowledged sufficient motive for the creation of fantasy assurances. Let us consider some of these aspects.

A complex of derivatives of the Christian idea of perfection proved to be the controlling symbolism in gnostic speculation. Clearly, an element of insecurity must be involved in this idea, which moves men to search for a firmer foundation for their existence in this world. It will therefore be necessary first to discuss faith in the Christian sense as the source of this insecurity.

In the Epistle to the Hebrews, faith is defined as the substance of things hoped for and the proof of things unseen. This is the definition that forms the basis for Thomas Aquinas' theological exposition of faith. The definition consists of two parts—an ontological and an epistemological proposition. The ontological proposition asserts that faith is the substance of things hoped for. The substance of these things subsists in nothing but this very faith, and not perhaps in its theological symbolism. The second proposition asserts that faith is the proof of things unseen. Again, proof lies in nothing but faith itself. This thread of faith, on which hangs all certainty regarding divine, transcendent being, is indeed very thin. Man is given nothing tangible. The substance and proof of the unseen are ascertained through nothing but faith, which man must obtain by the strength of his soul—in this psychological study we disregard the problem of grace. Not all men are capable of such spiritual stamina; most need institutional help, and even this is not always sufficient. We are confronted with the singular situation that Christian faith is so much the more threatened, the further it expands socially, the more it brings men under institutional control, and the more clearly its essence is articulated. This threat had reached the critical point in the high Middle Ages because of widespread social success. Christianity had in fact institutionally encompassed the men of Western society; and in the new urban culture, under the influence of the great religious orders, its essence had attained a high degree of clarity. Coincidentally with its greatness, its weakness became apparent: great masses of Christianized men who were not strong enough for the heroic adventure of faith became susceptible to ideas that could give them a greater degree of certainty about the meaning of their existence than faith. The reality of being as it is known in its truth by Christianity is difficult to bear, and the flight from clearly seen reality to gnostic constructs will probably always be a phenomenon of wide extent in civilizations that Christianity has permeated.

The temptation to fall from uncertain truth into certain untruth is stronger in the clarity of Christian faith than in other spiritual structures. But the absence of a secure hold on reality and the demanding spiritual strain are generally characteristic of border experiences in which man's knowledge of transcendent being, and thereby of the origin and meaning of mundane being, is constituted. This may be illustrated briefly in three examples taken from different cultural contexts—the Jewish, the Hellenic, and the Islamic.

In the Jewish sphere, faith responds to the revelation of God. The central experience of revelation is transmitted in Exodus 3, in the thornbush episode. God reveals himself in his nature to Moses with the expression, "I am who I am." As the formulation in the Epistle to the Hebrews is the basis of Thomas' theology of faith, so that in Exodus is the basis of his teaching on God. Again, one can say of the latter formulation only: That is all. In the contact the human soul in the world has with the beyond, nothing is discovered but the existence of God. Everything beyond this belongs to the realm of analogical-speculative deduction and mythic symbolization. Even in Moses' experience of revelation, we must observe that the thread on which hangs our knowledge of the order of being, its origin and meaning, is very thin. It was in fact so thin that it snapped, and the bulk of the people reverted to the old gods of polytheistic civilization. Furthermore, the prophet Jeremiah made the penetrating observation that nations in general do not desert their gods, although they are "false"; while Israel, who has the "true God," deserts Him. This unique case in the history of the peoples of the time attests perhaps most clearly to the phenomenon we just observed in connection with the experience of faith: with the refinement and clarification of the relationship between God and man, the moment of uncertainty, and with it the need for more solid certainty, is intensified. The example of Israel further shows that the lapse from faith by no means must result in this or that form of gnosis. If, experientially, the cultural conditions permit it, the need for certainty can also be satisfied by a reversion to a still vital polytheism.

The great demand on man's spiritual strength is clarified in the symbolism of the Last Judgment as Plato develops it in his *Gorgias*. To his sophist opponents, who operate with the ethic of worldly success of the man of power, Plato counters with the argument that "success" in life consists in standing before the judges of the dead. Before these judges the soul stands stripped of the husk of the body and the cloak of earthly status, in complete transparency. And life should be led in anticipation of this final transparency, *sub specie mortis,* rather than under the compulsions of the will to power and social status. What is being expressed symbolically in the Platonic myth, as in all myths of judgment, is the border experience of the examination of conscience. Over and above the normal testing of our actions against the standards of rational ethics, which is called conscience and which we as men perform, the experience of examination can be elaborated meditatively and expanded to the experience of standing in Judgment. Man knows that even the most conscientious self-examination is limited by the bounds of his humanity: breakdowns in judgment; on principle, incomplete knowledge of all the factors of the situation and of all the ramifications of action; and, above all, inadequate knowledge of his own ultimate motives, which reach into the unconscious. Proceeding by way of meditative experiment from this knowledge of the limitations of self-appraisal, one can imagine the situation in which a man is to be judged, not at a particular moment in a particular situation of his life and before himself alone, but on the basis of his entire life (which is completed only in death) and before an omniscient judge, before whom there is no longer any pleading of special points and no argument or defense is possible because everything, even the least and most remote, is already known. In this meditation at the border, all pro and con fall silent, and nothing remains but the silence of the judgment that the human being has spoken upon himself with his life.

Plato carried out this meditation—otherwise he could not have composed his myth of the judgment. But if we put ourselves in the situation in which he has his Socrates relate the myth to his sophist opponents and if we ask about the possibility of its having affected these hardboiled *Realpolitiker,* standing firmly in "life," then we must again doubt that many took it to heart and let their existence be formed by it—even though, while listening, they may have been profoundly touched for a moment. The meditation itself and, still more, existence in its tension would be unbearable for most men. At any rate, we find right in the gnostic mass movements a development of the idea of conscience that leads off in the opposite direction from the meditation at the border, toward worldliness. Conscience is readily invoked, even today, especially when a politician's immoral or criminal conduct is to be justified by having "followed his conscience" or by "being aware of his responsibilities."

But in this case conscience no longer means the testing of one's actions against the rational principles of ethics, but, on the contrary, the cutting off of rational debates and the stubborn, demonic persistence in actions that passion incites.

The Islamic prayer exercises that have developed since the ninth century will serve as the final example of a high demand in spiritual tension. Structurally, this meditation, which preceded prayer, is most closely related to the meditative experiment on which the Platonic myth of the Last Judgment is based. When I want to pray, says the rule, I go to the place where I wish to say my prayer. I sit still until I am composed. Then I stand up: the Kaaba is in front of me, paradise to my right, hell to my left, and the angel of death stands behind me. Then I say my prayer as if it were my last. And thus I stand, between hope and fear, not knowing whether God has received my prayer favorably or not. Perhaps, for the masses, this high spiritual clarity is made bearable through a connection with the neither high nor especially spiritual extension of God's realm by force of arms over the ecumene.

The gnostic mass movements of our time betray in their symbolism a certain derivation from Christianity and its experience of faith. The temptation to fall from a spiritual height that brings the element of uncertainty into final clarity down into the more solid certainty of world-immanent, sensible fulfillment, nevertheless, seems to be a general human problem. Cases of border experience, where the element of insecurity in the constitution of being becomes evident, were chosen from four different civilizational orbits to show that a typical phenomenon is involved in the modern mass movements, despite their historical uniqueness. Empirically, this insight will perhaps contribute something to the understanding of social processes in different civilizations. At any rate, we have managed theoretically to trace the phenomenon back to its ontic roots and to reduce it to ontological type concepts. And this is the task of science.